Holiday Recipes

By Barbara C. Jones

And

Sheryn R. Jones

Holiday Recipes

First Printing • July 1998
Second Printing • July 1999
Third Printing • April 2004

Holiday Treats Copyright © 1998 BJC Publication
Holiday Recipes Revised 2004 Copyright ©
Sheryn R. Jones, 2004, Highland Village, Texas

ISBN: 1-931294-22-4

Library of Congress Number: 2004109490

Illustrated by Nancy Murphy Griffith

Edited, Designed and Published in the
United States of America by
Cookbook Resources, LLC
541 Doubletree Drive
Highland Village, Texas 75077
Toll free 866-229-2665
www.cookbookresources.com
Manufactured in China

cookbook resources LLC
Bringing Family And Friends To The Table

Dedicated to a Loving

Husband and Father

Homer C. Jones

Table of Contents

*H*oliday *Recipes* is a cookbook that makes the holidays fun, even for the cook. It is a guide for traditional recipes but also includes new recipes that are sure to become traditions. Try the different breakfast breads and muffins, special salads, spreads and dips and unforgettable desserts. They are all here just for you to treat your family and guests to a celebration of the season.

Enjoy the sections on how to carve the turkey, how to trim the ham, how to make good use of the leftovers and how to make delicious food gifts such as *Spiced Pecans*.

Are you Planning an afternoon reception? You can't beat our *Very Special Coffee Punch* served with any of our cakes, pies, cookies or candies. They are guaranteed crowd- pleasers.

Informal get-togethers are fantastic with "finger foods" like *Hanky Panky Bites*, *Smoked Salmon Log*, *Oat Munchies*, *Almond Coconut Squares* or *Macadamia Candy*.

A traditional dinner becomes a feast with *Turkey and Dressing, Cranapple Wiggle* and *Holiday Lemon-Pecan Cake* that is heaven.

Start Christmas morning off with *Hidden Secret Muffins, Praline French Toast* and *Christmas Preserves*. You will receive praises galore.

When you get the nibbles try *Reindeer Rapture, Cherry-Pecan Slices* or any of our delicious cookies and candies. They will have you dreaming of sugarplums.

Enjoy the holidays, enjoy yourself and enjoy sharing our *Holiday Recipes* when entertaining family and friends.

Happy Holidays,

Barbara C. Jones and Sheryn R. Jones

Very Special Coffee Punch

I Promise – This Will Be a Hit!

1 (2 ounce) jar instant coffee
2 quarts hot water
2¼ cups sugar
2 quarts half-and-half
1 quart ginger ale, chilled
1 pint heavy cream, whipped
½ gallon French vanilla ice cream

Dissolve instant coffee in hot water and cool.

Add sugar and half-and-half, mix well and chill.

When ready to serve, pour coffee-sugar mixture in punch bowl, add chilled ginger ale, whipped cream and ice cream. Let some chunks of ice cream remain.

Yield: 60 (4 ounce) servings

Everyone will be back for seconds!

Holiday Party Punch

The almond extract really gives this punch a special taste!

3 cups sugar
2½ quarts water, divided
1 (6 ounce) package lemon gelatin
1 (3 ounce) can frozen orange juice concentrate, thawed
⅓ cup lemon juice
1 (46 ounce) can pineapple juice
3 tablespoons almond extract
2 quarts ginger ale, chilled

Combine sugar and 1 quart water. Heat until sugar dissolves.

Add gelatin and stir until it dissolves. Add fruit juices, remaining 1½ quarts water and almond extract and chill.

When ready to serve, place in punch bowl and add chilled ginger ale.

Serves 50.

Ruby Holiday Punch

*The cranapple juice in this punch really makes it a
"Christmas" special!*

2 (6 ounce) cans frozen orange juice concentrate, thawed
4 cups water
2 (46 ounce) cans red tropical punch
1 (46 ounce) can pineapple juice
1 (48 ounce) bottle cranapple juice
2 liters ginger ale, chilled

In 2-gallon bottles, combine orange juice, water, tropical punch,
pineapple juice and cranapple juice and stir well.

Chill and place in punch bowl.

Just before serving, add chilled ginger ale.

Makes 2 gallons.

Green Party Punch

This punch would also be a good one to use when the party is close to St. Patrick's Day!

1 (3 ounce) package lime gelatin
1 cup boiling water
1 (6 ounce) can frozen limeade, thawed
1 (6 ounce) can frozen lemonade, thawed
1 quart orange juice
1 quart pineapple juice
1 tablespoon almond extract
2 to 3 drops green food coloring
1 liter ginger ale, chilled

Dissolve lime gelatin and boiling water and stir well.

In 1-gallon bottle, combine dissolved gelatin, limeade, lemonade, orange juice, pineapple juice, almond extract and food coloring and chill.

When ready to serve, add chilled ginger ale.

Serves 32.

Reception Punch

4 cups sugar
6 cups water
5 ripe bananas, mashed
Juice of 2 lemons
1 (46 ounce) can pineapple juice
1 (6 once) can frozen undiluted orange juice, thawed
2 quarts ginger ale

Boil sugar and water for 3 minutes and cool.

Blend bananas with lemon juice and add pineapple and orange juice.

Combine all ingredients except ginger ale. Freeze in large container.

To serve, thaw 1½ hours, then add ginger ale. Punch will be slushy.

Serves 40.

Simple And Easy Punch
– But Very Good

Just chill bottles of Sparkling White Grape Juice. What could be easier than that!

Sparkling Cranberry Punch

Ice mold for punch bowl
Red food coloring (optional)
2 quarts cranberry juice cocktail
1 (6 ounce) can frozen lemonade, thawed
1 quart ginger ale, chilled

Pour water in mold for ice ring and add red food coloring to make mold brighter and prettier.

Mix cranberry juice and lemonade in pitcher. Chill until ready to serve.

When ready to serve, pour cranberry mixture into punch bowl, add chilled ginger ale and stir well.

Add decorative ice mold to punch bowl.

Serves 24.

Strawberry Spritzer

1 (10 ounce) package frozen strawberries in syrup, thawed
1 (24 ounce) bottle white grape juice, chilled
1 (12 ounce) can club soda, chilled

Process strawberries and syrup in blender until smooth, but stop once to scrape down sides.

Mix strawberry puree and white grape juice and add chilled club soda.

Serves 7.

Champagne Punch

This makes a good "wedding reception" punch, too!

1 bottle rose wine
1 cup honey
2 (6 ounce) cans frozen orange juice, undiluted
3 liters champagne

Chill all ingredients and mix.

Pour into a beautiful punch bowl.

Kahlua

3 cups hot water
1 cup instant coffee granules
4 cups sugar
1 quart vodka
1 vanilla bean, split

In large saucepan combine hot water and coffee and mix well.

Add sugar and bring to boil. Boil 2 minutes, turn off heat and cool.

Add vodka and vanilla bean. Pour into bottle or jar, set for 30 days before serving. Shake occasionally.

Tip: If you happen to have some of the Mexican vanilla, you can make "instant" kahlua by using 3 tablespoons of Mexican vanilla instead of the vanilla bean and you do not have to wait 30 days.

Amaretto

3 cups sugar
2¼ cups water
1 pint vodka
3 tablespoons almond extract
1 tablespoon vanilla (not imitation)

Combine sugar and water in large saucepan. Bring mixture to a boil and reduce heat.

Simmer 5 minutes and stir occasionally. Remove from stove.

Add vodka, almond and vanilla and stir to mix well.

Store in airtight jars.

Dipper's Delight

This is a so good you'll want to make it into a sandwich!

1 (8 ounce) package cream cheese, softened
2 tablespoons milk
1 (2.5 ounce) package smoked, sliced, pressed pastrami, cut into very fine pieces
3 green onions with tops, finely sliced
3 tablespoons finely chopped green pepper
¼ teaspoon black pepper
⅓ cup mayonnaise
½ cup chopped pecans
½ teaspoon hot sauce
¼ teaspoon garlic powder
½ teaspoon seasoned salt
½ teaspoon Italian herbs

In mixing bowl, whip cream cheese and milk until creamy.

Add remaining ingredients, mix well and chill.

Serve with crackers.

Holiday Crabmeat Spread

1 (8 ounce) package cream cheese, softened
1 (3 ounce) package cream cheese, softened
1 bunch green onions with tops, finely chopped
1 teaspoon lemon juice
¾ teaspoon seasoned salt
½ teaspoon Worcestershire
1 tablespoon dried parsley flakes
2 (6½ ounce) cans crabmeat, drained, flaked
1 cup cocktail sauce
½ cup chopped pecans

In mixing bowl, combine cream cheese, onion, lemon juice, seasoned salt, Worcestershire and parsley flakes. Beat until fluffy.

Spread on bottom of 9-inch glass pie plate or similar pretty serving platter.

Flake crabmeat and distribute evenly over cream cheese.

Spoon cocktail sauce over crabmeat and sprinkle with pecans. Chill until ready to serve.

Serve with crackers.

Hanky-Panky Bites

1 pound ground pork sausage
1 pound lean ground beef
1 pound mild Mexican processed cheese, cubed
1 teaspoon garlic powder
1 teaspoon oregano
½ teaspoon seasoned salt
1 tablespoon Worcestershire
Loaf of square white sandwich bread
Paprika
1 (6 ounce) bottle stuffed green olives

Brown meats, stir until crumbly and drain.

Add cheese to meat, stir well and cook over low heat until cheese melts.

Add seasonings and Worcestershire, mix well and remove from heat.

Trim crusts from bread and cut each slice into fourths.

Spread about a tablespoon of meat mixture on bread squares, place on cookie sheet and sprinkle paprika on squares.

Place ½ of an olive (cut side up) in middle of each square. Punch olive down firmly into meat so it will stay.

After they are frozen, take off cookie sheet and place in baggies for the freezer.

When ready to serve, take as many as you want and bake at 350° for 12 to 15 minutes.

Cocky-Broccoli Cheese Dip

1 (10 ounce) package frozen chopped broccoli, thawed, drained
2 tablespoons butter
2 ribs celery, chopped
1 small onion, finely chopped
1 (1 pound) box mild Mexican processed cheese, cubed

Make sure broccoli is thoroughly thawed and drained. (If you will place broccoli between several paper towels and squeeze, it will help get the water out).

Place butter in large saucepan and saute broccoli, celery and onion at medium heat for about 5 minutes and stir several times.

Add cheese and heat just until cheese melts and serve hot with chips.

Spinach-Crab Balls

1 tablespoon butter

1 onion, minced

2 (10 ounce) packages frozen chopped spinach, thawed, well drained and patted dry

4 eggs

2 tablespoons flour

4 slices bacon, cooked, crumbled

½ cup (1 stick) butter, softened

1 (7½ ounce) can crabmeat, drained, flaked

2 cups seasoned stuffing, crumbled

¼ teaspoon pepper

½ teaspoon salt

½ teaspoon dillweed

¼ teaspoon garlic powder

Preheat oven to 325°.

Melt butter in skillet, stir in onion and saute.

Mix thoroughly with remaining ingredients, form into 1½-inch balls and place on baking sheet.

Bake at 325° for 15 minutes and serve warm. These can be served plain or with sweet-and-hot mustard. (See page 175.)

Tip: *If you want to make ahead and bake when you are ready to serve, just freeze spinach balls on baking sheet and then remove to a plastic bag to store frozen.*

Spinach-Cheese Squares

¼ cup (½ stick) butter
1 cup flour
3 eggs
1 cup milk
1 teaspoon salt
1 teaspoon baking powder
1 teaspoon dry mustard
2 (10 ounce) packages frozen spinach, thawed, drained, squeezed dry
8 ounces mozzarella cheese, shredded
8 ounces cheddar cheese, shredded

Preheat oven to 350°.

Melt butter in 9 x 13-inch baking dish in oven.

In large mixing bowl, combine flour, eggs, milk, salt, baking powder and mustard and mix well.

Add spinach and both cheeses and pour into pan.

Bake at 350° for 30 minutes. When set, cut into squares and serve warm. This may be reheated.

Great Grape Meatballs

1½ pounds lean ground beef
3 eggs
1 teaspoon dried parsley flakes
½ teaspoon garlic powder
1 teaspoon seasoned salt
½ teaspoon black pepper
½ teaspoon dried cilantro leaves
5 slices bread, crumbled in food processor
1 (16 ounce) jar grape jam (not jelly)
1 (12 ounce) jar chili sauce

Combine beef, eggs, parsley, garlic powder, seasoned salt, pepper, cilantro leaves and breadcrumbs.

Roll into ¾-inch meatballs and brown in skillet.

Combine jam and chili sauce in large slow cooker or large saucepan.

Heat, add meatballs to slow cooker and simmer for 1 hour.

Serve hot in chafing dish or you can leave in slow cooker if the party is not really formal.

Tinsel Tenderloin

1½ pounds whole pork tenderloin
¼ cup dry white wine
1 teaspoon marjoram leaves
1 teaspoon dried rosemary leaves
¼ teaspoon garlic powder
¼ teaspoon black pepper
½ teaspoon salt
¼ cup (½ stick) butter, melted

Preheat oven to 450°.

Place tenderloin in baking pan.

Combine wine, marjoram, rosemary, garlic powder, black pepper and salt, blend well and pour over meat.

Cover and marinate at room temperature for 20 minutes. Remove pork from marinade and place on baking sheet.

Pour butter over tenderloin. Roast on middle rack of oven for 30 minutes and baste meat thoroughly every 10 minutes.

If meat has not browned a little, turn broiler on just until meat browns slightly.

Remove from oven and cool to room temperature.

Slice meat very thin to serve. Serve on slices of party rye bread, if you like.

Smoked-Salmon Log

This is so good, you'll make it all year long!

1 (15 ounce) can red salmon
1 (8 ounce) package cream cheese, softened
1 tablespoon lemon juice
2 tablespoons grated onion
¼ teaspoon salt
¼ teaspoon liquid smoke
6 tablespoons very finely crushed crackers
1 cup very finely chopped pecans
3 tablespoons minced fresh parsley

Drain salmon, remove skin and bones and flake with fork.

In mixing bowl, beat cream cheese and lemon juice.

Add onion, salt, liquid smoke, crackers and salmon and mix. (Add another spoonful of cracker crumbs if mixture seems too sticky.)

Chill several hours or overnight.

Spread out a piece of wax paper and put a very light coat of flour on it. Make a roll with salmon mixture and roll in pecans and parsley mixture.

Roll onto another piece of wax paper to lift roll. Chill several hours and serve with crackers.

Sweet-And-Sour Sausage Balls

1 pound hot ground pork sausage
1 pound mild ground pork sausage
2 eggs
½ teaspoon seasoned salt
2 cups soft breadcrumbs

Sauce:
1 (12 ounce) bottle cocktail sauce
¾ cup packed brown sugar
½ cup wine vinegar
½ cup soy sauce

Mix sausage, eggs, seasoned salt and breadcrumbs and form into small balls.

Brown sausage balls and drain.

Combine all sauce ingredients and pour over sausage balls.

Simmer uncovered for about 1 hour.

You could also use a slow cooker to simmer the sausage balls and serve in the slow cooker if it is an informal occasion.

Wonder Dip

This is really a different, unique taste!

⅓ cup finely chopped green onions
½ cup very finely cut broccoli (tiny florets)
1 (8 ounce) can water chestnuts, drained, coarsely chopped
¾ cup mayonnaise
¾ cup sour cream
1 (2.7 ounce) jar crystallized ginger, finely chopped
½ cup finely chopped pecans
½ teaspoon salt
2 tablespoons soy sauce

Prepare a day before serving and chill.

Mix all ingredients. Serve with wheat crackers.

Crab-Artichoke Spread

1½ cups fresh parmesan cheese
1 (14 ounce) can artichokes, drained, chopped
1½ cups mayonnaise
½ cup finely minced onion
½ teaspoon Worcestershire
¼ cup fine breadcrumbs
⅛ teaspoon garlic powder
2 drops Tabasco, optional
1 (6 ounce) can crabmeat, drained, flaked
Paprika

Preheat oven to 350°.

Mix parmesan cheese, artichokes, mayonnaise, onion, Worcestershire, breadcrumbs, garlic powder, Tabasco and crabmeat.

Spread onto buttered 9-inch glass pie plate and sprinkle a good amount of paprika over spread.

Bake for 20 minutes and serve with crackers.

Green Eyes

4 large dill pickles
4 slices boiled ham
Light cream cheese
Black pepper
Garlic powder

Dry pickles with paper towels and set aside.

Lightly coat one side of ham slices with cream cheese and sprinkle a little pepper and a little garlic powder on each slice.

Roll pickle in slice of ham coated with cream cheese mixture, chill and cut into circles.

Seafood Spread

1 (8 ounce) package cream cheese, softened
⅓ cup mayonnaise
⅓ cup sour cream
3 hard-boiled eggs, mashed
1 (8 ounce) can crabmeat, drained, flaked
2 (8 ounce) cans tiny shrimp, drained, chopped
¼ onion, very finely chopped
1 rib celery, very finely chopped
1 teaspoon creole seasoning
Several dashes hot sauce

Combine cream cheese, mayonnaise, sour cream and hard-boiled eggs in mixing bowl and beat until fairly smooth.

Add crabmeat, shrimp, onion, celery, creole seasoning and hot sauce and mix well. Serve with crackers.

Tip: This may also be used as a dip or to make good sandwiches.

Spicy Party Spread

1 cup chopped pecans
1 tablespoon butter, melted
2 (8 ounce) packages cream cheese, softened
1 (1.3 ounce) package taco seasoning
⅔ cup shredded cheddar cheese
1 cup picante sauce
1 bunch green onions with tops, chopped

Preheat oven to 275°.

Bake pecans in shallow pan with butter for about 25 minutes.

In mixing bowl, beat cream cheese, taco seasoning and cheddar cheese and stir in picante sauce, pecans and onions.

Spoon into greased 9-inch glass pie plate.

Bake, covered, at 325° for 15 minutes. Serve hot and spread on crackers.

Elegant Crab Dip

1 (6 ½ ounce) can white crabmeat, drained
1 (8 ounce) package cream cheese
½ cup (1 stick) butter

In saucepan, combine crabmeat, cream cheese and butter, heat and mix thoroughly.

Transfer to hot chafing dish and serve with chips.

Deviled-Egg Spread

A fun way to use this spread is to quarter small green bell peppers and fill with Deviled Egg Spread.

3 hard-boiled eggs, mashed
1 (3 ounce) package cream cheese, softened
4 ounces Monterrey Jack cheese, grated
½ cup mayonnaise
½ teaspoon prepared mustard
¼ teaspoon salt
½ teaspoon white pepper
¾ cup finely grated chopped pecans
1 (4 ounce) can chopped green chilies, drained

In mixing bowl, combine eggs, cream cheese, Jack cheese, mayonnaise, mustard, salt and pepper and beat well.

Add chopped pecans and green chilies, mix and chill.

Hot Artichoke Spread

1 (14 ounce) can artichoke hearts, drained, chopped
1 (4 ounce) can chopped green chilies, drained
1 cup mayonnaise
1 cup grated mozzarella cheese
¼ teaspoon white pepper
½ teaspoon garlic salt
Paprika

Preheat oven to 300°.

Remove any spikes or tough leaves from artichoke hearts.

Combine all ingredients and mix well.

Place in 9-inch baking dish sprayed with vegetable cooking spray and sprinkle paprika over top.

Bake at 300° for 30 minutes. Serve warm with tortilla chips or crackers.

Southwestern Dip

*Who would ever expect to put corn and walnuts in a dip –
try it, it's great!*

2 (8 ounce) packages cream cheese, softened
¼ cup lime juice
1 tablespoon cumin
1 teaspoon salt
½ to 1 teaspoon cayenne pepper
1 (8 ounce) can whole kernel corn, drained
1 cup chopped walnuts
1 (4 ounce) can chopped green chilies, drained
3 green onions with tops, chopped

In mixing bowl, whip cream cheese until fluffy and beat in lime juice, cumin, salt and cayenne pepper.

Stir in corn, walnuts, green chilies and onions and chill. Serve with tortilla chips.

Party Sausages

1 cup ketchup
1 cup plum jelly
1 tablespoon lemon juice
2 tablespoons prepared mustard
2 (5 ounce) packages tiny smoked sausages

In saucepan, combine all ingredients except sausages, heat and mix well.

Add sausages and simmer for 10 minutes. Serve with cocktail toothpicks.

Asparagus Rolls

20 thin slices white bread
1 (8 ounce) package cream cheese, softened
3 tablespoons butter, softened
1 egg
½ teaspoon seasoned salt
20 canned asparagus spears, drained
¾ cup (1½ sticks) butter, melted

Preheat oven to 400°.

Remove crusts from bread and flatten slices with rolling pin.

In mixing bowl combine cream cheese, butter, egg and seasoned salt. Spread mixture evenly over bread slices.

Place an asparagus spear on each one and roll up.

Dip in melted butter to coat all sides, place on cookie sheet and freeze until ready to bake.

Cut frozen rolls into thirds and bake for 15 minutes or until lightly browned. Serve immediately.

Horsey Shrimp Dip

1 (8 ounce) package cream cheese, softened
⅔ cup mayonnaise
1 tablespoon lemon juice
3 tablespoons creamy horseradish
¼ cup chili sauce
½ teaspoon creole seasoning
¼ teaspoon garlic powder
2 (8 ounce) cans shrimp, drained
2 green onions with tops, chopped

In mixing bowl, combine cream cheese, mayonnaise, lemon juice, horseradish, chili sauce, creole seasoning and garlic powder and blend well.

Chop shrimp and onions, add to cream cheese mixture, blend and chill. Serve with chips.

Sassy Onion Dip

1 (8 ounce) package cream cheese, softened
1 (8 ounce) carton sour cream
½ cup chili sauce
1 (1 ounce) package dry onion soup mix

In mixing bowl, beat cheese until fluffy.

Add remaining ingredients, mix well, cover and chill.

Serve with strips of raw zucchini, celery, carrots or turnips.

Florentine Dip

1 (10 ounce) package frozen, chopped spinach, thawed
1 (8 ounce) package cream cheese, softened
⅔ cup mayonnaise
2 hard-boiled eggs, finely chopped
¼ teaspoon pepper
¾ teaspoon seasoned salt

Drain spinach by using several sheets of paper towels to blot spinach very dry. (Do not cook.)

In mixing bowl, combine cream cheese, mayonnaise, eggs, pepper and seasoned salt and beat.

Add spinach, mix and chill. Serve with vegetable dippers.

Apricot-Bread Extraordinaire

This is "it" for apricot lovers!

3 cups flour
1½ teaspoons baking soda
½ teaspoon salt
2 cups sugar
1½ cups oil
4 eggs
1 teaspoon vanilla
1 (5 ounce) can evaporated milk
1¼ cups apricot-butter
1¼ cups chopped pecans

Apricot butter:
1¼ cups finely chopped apricots
1 cup sugar

Preheat oven to 350°.

Mix flour, baking soda and salt.

Add sugar, oil, eggs, vanilla and evaporated milk and mix thoroughly. Add apricot butter and pecans and blend.

Pour into 2 greased, floured loaf pans and bake for 1 hour and 5 to 10 minutes or until loaf tests done.

To make apricot-butter, soak dry apricots overnight in water, covered. Add sugar and simmer 10 minutes or until soft. Cool completely before adding to recipe.

Glazed-Lemon Bread

½ cup shortening
1 cup sugar
2 eggs
1½ cups flour
1 teaspoon baking powder
Pinch of salt
½ cup milk
1½ teaspoons lemon extract
Rind of 2 lemons, grated
½ cup chopped pecans

Glaze:
Juice of 2 lemons
¼ cup sugar

Preheat oven to 325°.

Cream shortening and sugar, add eggs and beat thoroughly.

Sift flour, baking powder and salt. Add to creamed mixture alternately with milk. Add lemon extract and grated lemon rind. Fold in chopped pecans.

Pour into greased, floured loaf pan and bake for 60 to 65 minutes. Test with toothpick.

For glaze, combine lemon juice and sugar in saucepan and bring to a boil.

Pour over hot bread while still in pan. Use toothpick to pierce bread so glaze will run into loaf.

Butternut Bread

This bread is a little more trouble, but well worth it. It is different, delicious and very good toasted for breakfast.

1 butternut squash
2½ cups flour
2 teaspoons baking powder
1 teaspoon baking soda
1 teaspoon cinnamon
½ teaspoon ground allspice
½ teaspoon ground ginger
½ teaspoon ground nutmeg
½ teaspoon salt
¾ cup (1½ sticks) butter, softened
1 cup granulated sugar
½ cup packed brown sugar
2 eggs
1 (8 ounce) carton sour cream
1 teaspoon vanilla
1 cup chopped pecans

Trim ends off squash and cut in half lengthwise. Scoop out and discard seeds. Cut squash into 2-inch pieces, leaving skin on.

Steam squash about 25 minutes until completely tender and drain well.

When squash is cool enough to handle, use spoon to scoop flesh away from skin. Mash squash with fork and set aside.

Preheat oven to 350°.

(continued on next page)

(continued)

Sift flour, baking powder, baking soda, spices and salt in bowl and set aside.

In mixing bowl, cream butter and both sugars until smooth. Add eggs and beat well.

Add sour cream, vanilla and 1 cup of butternut squash (discard remaining) and mix well.

Stir in dry ingredients just until combined. Stir in pecans. Pour into greased and floured loaf pan.

Bake for 1 hour and 10 to 15 minutes or until a toothpick comes out clean. Cool in pan 15 minutes, then turn onto rack and continue cooling.

Mincemeat Bread

Wonderful!

1¾ cups flour
1¼ cups sugar
2½ teaspoons baking powder
½ teaspoon salt
2 eggs, beaten
1 teaspoon vanilla
1½ cups prepared mincemeat
¾ cup chopped pecans
⅓ cup shortening, melted

Glaze:
1 cup powdered sugar
1 tablespoon milk
¼ cup finely chopped pecans

Preheat oven to 350°.

In large bowl combine flour, sugar, baking powder and salt.

In medium bowl combine eggs, vanilla, mincemeat and pecans and mix well. Stir in melted shortening and mix quickly. (Batter will be stiff.)

Pour egg mixture into dry ingredients and stir only enough to moisten flour. Spoon batter into greased and floured pan.

Bake for 1 hour or until toothpick inserted in center comes out clean. Cool 15 minutes, remove from pan and cool completely.

Mix powdered sugar and milk and stir until smooth. Stir in pecans and spread over top of loaf.

Slice bread, toast and spread a little butter on each slice.

Jingle Bread

Yes, the sausage is right in the bread! A slice or two,
warmed or toasted makes a great breakfast!

¾ cup raisins
1 pound hot ground sausage
1½ cups packed light brown sugar
1½ cups sugar
2 eggs
1 cup chopped pecans
3 cups flour
1 teaspoon ginger
1 teaspoon allspice
1 teaspoon cinnamon
1 teaspoon baking powder
1 teaspoon baking soda
1 cup cold coffee

Preheat oven to 350°.

In saucepan cover raisins with water, simmer for 5 minutes and drain.

Combine raw sausage, sugars and eggs, then stir in pecans and raisins.

Combine flour, spices and baking powder in separate bowl.

Stir soda into coffee, blend coffee into flour mixture and stir all into sausage mixture. (This is when you have fun mixing with your hands.)

Pour into 2 greased and floured loaf pans. Bake for 1 hour and 10 minutes or until bread tests done. Chill.

Blueberry-Lemon Bread

Wonderful toasted for breakfast!

1¾ cups flour
1 teaspoon baking powder
¼ teaspoon salt
6 tablespoons (¾ stick) butter, softened
1 cup sugar
2 eggs
2 teaspoons grated lemon peel
½ cup milk
1½ cups frozen blueberries, thawed, well drained
½ cup sugar
3 tablespoons lemon juice

Preheat oven to 350°.

Combine flour, baking powder and salt in small bowl and set aside.

In mixing bowl, use electric mixer to cream butter with sugar until mixture is light and fluffy.

Add eggs, one at a time, and beat well after each addition. Add lemon peel and mix in dry ingredients, alternately with milk, beginning and ending with dry ingredients. Fold in blueberries.

Spoon batter into greased and floured loaf pan.

Bake at 350° for 1 hour and 5 minutes or until toothpick comes out clean.

During last 15 minutes of baking time, bring ½ cup sugar and 3 tablespoons lemon juice to boil in small saucepan and stir until sugar dissolves.

(continued on next page)

(continued)

When loaf is done and still hot, pierce top several times with toothpick.

Pour hot lemon mixture over loaf while still in pan. Cool 30 minutes on rack.

Turn bread out of pan and cool completely on rack.

Caramel Rolls

9 tablespoons butter, softened, divided
1 cup packed light brown sugar
¼ cup water
½ cup chopped pecans
2 (8 ounce) cans refrigerated crescent dinner rolls
¼ cup sugar
2 teaspoons cinnamon

Preheat oven to 375°.

In ungreased 9 x 13-inch pan, melt 5 tablespoons butter in oven. Stir in brown sugar, water and pecans and set aside.

Separate each can of roll dough in 4 rectangles. Pinch perforations together to seal.

Spread with 4 tablespoons softened butter. Combine sugar and cinnamon and sprinkle over dough.

Starting at shorter side, roll up each rectangle and cut each roll into 4 slices, making 32 pieces. Place in prepared pan.

Bake at 375° for 20 to 25 minutes or until golden brown. Invert immediately to remove from pan and serve warm.

Strawberry Bread

Great for finger food at parties or as sandwiches with cream cheese and pecans.

3 cups flour
1 teaspoon baking soda
1 teaspoon cinnamon
½ teaspoon salt
2 cups sugar
2 (10 ounce) cartons frozen strawberries, thawed
1¼ cups oil
4 eggs, beaten
1 teaspoon red food coloring

Preheat oven to 350°.

Combine flour, baking soda, cinnamon, salt and sugar in mixing bowl.

With spoon, make a "well" in dry ingredients, add strawberries, oil and eggs and mix well. Add food coloring and mix well.

Pour into 2 greased and floured loaf pans.

Bake at 350° for 1 hour.

Applesauce-Pecan Bread

1 cup sugar
1 cup applesauce
⅓ cup oil
2 eggs
2 tablespoons milk
1 teaspoon almond extract
2 cups flour
1 teaspoon baking soda
½ teaspoon baking powder
¾ teaspoon cinnamon
¼ teaspoon salt
¼ teaspoon ground nutmeg
¾ cup chopped pecans

Topping:
½ cup chopped pecans
½ teaspoon cinnamon
½ cup packed brown sugar

Preheat oven to 350°.

Combine sugar, applesauce, oil, eggs, milk and almond extract and mix well.

Combine all dry ingredients, add to sugar mixture and mix well. Fold in pecans.

Pour into greased and floured loaf pan.

For topping, combine pecans, cinnamon and brown sugar. Sprinkle over batter.

Bake at 350° for 1 hour and 5 minutes. Test for doneness and cool on rack.

Hidden Secret Muffins
These are what my Daddy would have called "Larripin good"!

Filling:
1 (8 ounce) package cream cheese, softened
1 egg
⅓ cup sugar
1 tablespoon grated orange rind

Muffin:
1 cup (2 sticks) butter, softened
1¾ cups sugar
3 eggs
3 cups flour
2 teaspoons baking powder
1 cup milk
1 teaspoon almond extract
1 cup chopped, almonds toasted

Preheat oven to 375°.

Beat cream cheese, egg, sugar and orange rind and set aside.

Cream butter and sugar until light and fluffy. Add eggs one at a time, beating after each addition.

Mix flour and baking powder. Add flour mixture and milk alternately to butter-sugar mixture, beginning and ending with flour mixture. Add almond extract and fold in almonds.

Fill 26 lightly greased muffin tins half full with muffin batter. Spoon about 1 heaping tablespoon of filling in each muffin tin and top fill each with muffin batter.

Bake muffins at 375° for 20 to 25 minutes or until muffin just bounces back when pressed or until they are lightly browned.

Applesauce-Spice Muffins

1 cup (2 sticks) butter, softened
1 cup packed brown sugar
1 cup granulated sugar
2 eggs
1¾ cups applesauce
2 teaspoons cinnamon
1 teaspoon allspice
½ teaspoon ground cloves
½ teaspoon salt
2 teaspoons baking soda
3½ cups flour
1½ cups chopped pecans

Preheat oven to 375°.

Cream butter with both sugars.

Add eggs, applesauce, cinnamon, allspice, cloves, salt, baking soda and flour and mix well. Add pecans and stir well.

Pour into 28 greased muffin tins or pans with paper liners.

Bake at 375° for 15 minutes.

Tip: See page 172 for instructions to toast almonds.

Apricot-Pineapple Muffins

This is a winner!

⅓ cup very finely cut dried apricots
½ cup (1 stick) butter, softened
1 cup sugar
1 egg
1 (8 ounce) can crushed pineapple with juice
1¼ cups flour
½ teaspoon baking soda
½ teaspoon salt
1 cup quick-rolled oats

Preheat oven to 350°.

(Cut apricots with kitchen scissors.)

With mixer, cream butter and sugar, add egg and pineapple and beat well.

Add all dry ingredients, mix well and fold in apricots.

Spoon into well greased muffin tins or use the paper liners.

Bake at 350° for 20 minutes.

Makes 12 muffins.

Pimento-Cheese Biscuits

2 cups flour
3 teaspoons baking powder
2 tablespoons sugar
1 teaspoon salt
A scant ⅛ teaspoon cayenne pepper
1½ cups shredded sharp cheddar cheese
¼ cup (½ stick) butter
4 tablespoons shortening
1 (2 ounce) jar chopped pimento, drained
¼ cup finely chopped green bell pepper
½ cup plus 2 tablespoons milk

Preheat oven to 400°.

Combine flour, baking powder, sugar, salt and cayenne pepper. Add cheese and mix well.

Cut butter and shortening into flour mixture with pastry blender or fork until consistency of coarse cornmeal.

Add pimento and green pepper. Make a well in dry ingredients and add milk.

Using a fork, stir to combine until mixture forms a ball. (You may need a little extra milk if it seems to dry to roll out.)

Turn dough onto a floured surface, roll out to ½-inch thickness and cut into 2-inch rounds.

Bake biscuits on ungreased cookie sheet at 400° for 12 to 15 minutes.

Eagle Yeast Bread

8 cups sifted flour, divided
1 tablespoon sugar
1 tablespoon salt
2 yeast cakes
1 (14 ounce) can sweetened condensed milk
⅓ cup oil

Preheat oven to 350°.

Combine 6 cups flour, sugar and salt and set aside.

Soften yeast in small amount of warm water. Add sweetened condensed milk, oil and enough warm water to measure 4 cups and mix well.

Add to flour mixture and mix well. Add remaining 2 cups flour and mix well.

Knead 10 minutes. Place in greased bowl and turn out onto greased surface.

Let rise, covered, for 1½ to 2 hours or until doubled in size.

Divide into 3 portions. Place in 3 greased loaf pans. Let rise 40 minutes.

Bake at 350° approximately 40 minutes. Brush with melted butter.

Buttermilk Rolls

2 yeast cakes
¼ cup warm water
1½ cups lukewarm buttermilk
3 tablespoons sugar
¼ cup oil
4½ cups flour
½ teaspoon baking soda
1 teaspoon salt

Preheat oven to 400°.

Soak yeast in warm water. Add warm buttermilk, sugar and oil.

Sift into this mixture flour, baking soda and salt. Form into dough and knead 10 minutes.

Shape into rolls and place in 2 greased pie pans. Let rise 30 to 45 minutes.

Bake at 400° for 15 to 20 minutes. Brush with melted butter.

Yields 1½ to 2 dozen rolls.

Crunchy Bread Sticks

You won't believe how good these are!

1 package hot dog buns
1 cup (2 sticks) butter, melted
Garlic powder
Paprika
Parmesan cheese

Preheat oven to 225°.

Take each half bun and slice in half lengthwise.

Use a pastry brush to butter all bread sticks and sprinkle a light amount of garlic powder and just a few sprinkles of paprika and parmesan cheese.

Place on cookie sheet and bake at 225° for about 45 minutes.

Mincemeat-Crumb Coffee Cake

Topping:
2 tablespoons flour
⅓ cup sugar
1½ teaspoons cinnamon
2 tablespoons butter

Cake:
1½ cups flour
¾ cup sugar
2 teaspoons baking powder
½ teaspoon salt
1 egg
½ cup milk
3 tablespoons butter, melted, cooled
1 cup prepared mincemeat
½ cup chopped pecans

Preheat oven to 375°.

Grease and flour 10-inch, deep-dish, pie plate.

For topping, mix dry ingredients, cut in butter until mixture becomes crumbly and set aside.

In mixing bowl, mix flour, sugar, baking powder and salt.

Beat egg with milk and melted butter. Add egg mixture to flour mixture and stir until smooth. Stir in mincemeat and pecans.

Spread batter into prepared pan and sprinkle with topping.

Bake at 375° for about 40 minutes or until tester comes out clean. Serve warm.

Good Morning Coffee Cake

2⅓ cups flour
1½ cups sugar
¾ teaspoon salt
¾ cup shortening
2 teaspoons baking powder
¾ cup milk
2 eggs
1 teaspoon vanilla
1 (3 ounce) package cream cheese, softened
1 (14 ounce) can sweetened condensed milk
⅓ cup lemon juice
1 (20 ounce) can peach pie filling, cut each peach slice into
    3 chunks
2 teaspoons cinnamon
¾ cup chopped pecans

Preheat oven to 350°.

In mixing bowl, combine flour, sugar and salt and cut in shortening until crumbly. Set aside 1 cup crumb mixture. To remaining crumb mixture, add baking powder, milk, eggs and vanilla. Beat on medium speed for 2 minutes.

Spread in greased, floured 9 x 13- inch baking dish. Bake at 350° for 25 minutes.

In another bowl, beat cream cheese and condensed milk until fluffy and gradually fold in lemon juice, peach pie filling and cinnamon. Spoon this mixture over hot cake.

Add pecans to remaining crumb mixture and sprinkle on top of cake.

Bake another 25 minutes. Let set 10 minutes before serving. Serve warm.

Breakfast Bake

1 pound hot ground sausage, cooked, crumbled
2 tablespoons dried onion flakes
1 cup grated cheddar cheese
1 cup biscuit mix
¼ teaspoon salt
¼ teaspoon pepper
4 eggs
2 cups milk

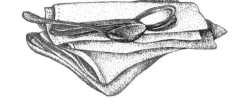

Preheat oven to 350°.

Place cooked, crumbled sausage in 9 x 13-inch glass baking dish sprayed with vegetable cooking spray. Sprinkle with onion flakes and cheese.

In mixing bowl, combine biscuit mix, salt, pepper and eggs and beat well. Add milk and stir until fairly smooth. Pour over sausage mixture.

Bake at 350° for 35 minutes.

Tips: *If you want to make one day and cook the next morning, just keep chilled before cooking. To cook the next morning, add an extra 5 minutes to cooking time because it is chilled. Serves 8.*

For a brunch, add 1 (8 ounce) can whole kernel corn, drained.

Quesadilla Pie

1 (4 ounce) can chopped green chilies, drained
½ pound ground sausage, cooked, drained
2 cups grated cheddar cheese
3 eggs, well beaten
1½ cups milk
¾ cup biscuit mix
Hot salsa

Preheat oven to 350°.

Spray a 9-inch pie pan with vegetable cooking spray.

Sprinkle green chilies in pie pan and add cooked sausage and cheddar cheese.

In separate bowl, mix eggs, milk and biscuit mix. Pour over chilies, sausage and cheese.

Bake at 350° for 30 minutes. Serve with salsa on top of each slice.

Serves 6.

Homemade Egg-Substitute

6 egg whites
¼ cup instant nonfat dry milk powder
2 teaspoons water
2 teaspoons oil
¼ teaspoon ground turmeric

Combine all ingredients in electric blender and process 30 seconds and chill. (¼ cup is the equivalent to one egg.)

Quick Holiday Breakfast

1 (8 ounce) package crescent dinner rolls
1 pound hot pork sausage, cooked, drained
5 eggs, beaten
¾ cup milk
½ teaspoon salt
¼ teaspoon black pepper
1 (8 ounce) package shredded mozzarella cheese

Preheat oven to 350°.

Line 9 x 13-inch baking dish with crescent rolls, pressing seams together and cover with sausage.

In medium bowl, combine remaining ingredients and pour over sausage.

Bake at 350° for 30 minutes. Let stand 5 minutes before serving.

Tip: This may be frozen before baking, placed in refrigerator the night before serving and baked the next morning. Add 5 minutes to baking time because it will be chilled.

Rise-And-Shine Eggs

2 cups finely chopped ham
1 cup shredded Monterrey Jack cheese
½ cup shredded cheddar cheese
1 tablespoon flour
8 eggs
1 cup milk
Salsa

Preheat oven to 350°.

Grease 9 x 13-inch glass baking dish. Sprinkle ham evenly over bottom, then sprinkle with both cheeses. Sprinkle flour over cheeses.

With back of large spoon, slightly hollow 8 places for eggs (away from the edge of glass).

Break each egg into small cup, pour one at a time, into indentations and lightly break yolks with tip of knife.

Pour milk on top and bake at 350° for about 30 minutes (depending on preference for soft or hard-boiled eggs).

Serve with salsa on the side.

Sausage-Apple Ring

2 pounds ground pork sausage
1½ cups crushed cracker crumbs
2 eggs, slightly beaten
½ cup milk
¼ cup minced onion
1 cup finely chopped apple
Scrambled eggs

Preheat oven to 350°.

Thoroughly combine sausage, cracker crumbs, eggs, milk, onion and apple.

Press lightly into greased ring mold and turn out into a shallow baking pan or sheet cake pan.

Bake at 350° for 50 minutes.

Drain well before placing on serving platter. Fill center with scrambled eggs and serve immediately. (It will take about a dozen eggs to fill the center.)

Tip: Bake this partially for 30 minutes, then drain fat, refrigerate and finish baking when ready to serve.

Praline French Toast

8 large eggs, beaten
1½ cups half-and-half cream
4 tablespoons brown sugar
¼ teaspoon salt
2 teaspoons vanilla
8 thick slices French bread or the thick square bread
½ cup (1 stick) butter
¾ cup packed brown sugar
⅔ cup maple syrup
1 cup chopped pecans

In small bowl, combine eggs, half-and-half, brown sugar, salt and vanilla. Pour half into 9 x 13-inch pan.

Cover with bread slices and top with remaining egg mixture. Cover and chill overnight.

Before serving, preheat oven to 350°.

In another 9 x 13-inch glass baking dish, melt butter and stir in brown sugar, maple syrup and pecans.

Cover butter mixture with soaked bread slices and bake at 350° for 30 to 35 minutes until puffed and brown.

If not slightly browned, turn on broiler for a minute or two. Cut into squares and serve immediately.

Serves 8.

Holiday Salad

1 (6 ounce) package lime gelatin
1 (8 ounce) can crushed pineapple, drained, reserve juice
Juice from pineapple plus water to make 1 cup
1 (8 ounce) package cream cheese, softened
1 cup miniature marshmallows
1 (8 ounce) carton whipped topping
1 (6 ounce) package raspberry gelatin
1 cup boiling water
1 (12 ounce) package frozen raspberries, thawed
1 (8 ounce) can crushed pineapple with juice

Dissolve lime gelatin in large mixing bowl with 1 cup boiling pineapple juice and water.

Add cream cheese and beat on slow speed of mixer. Fold in marshmallows and pineapple.

Chill in refrigerator about 30 minutes and fold in whipped topping.

Pour into 9 x 13-inch glass dish sprayed with vegetable cooking spray and chill until set.

In separate bowl, dissolve raspberry gelatin with boiling water.

Add raspberries and crushed pineapple and pour over first layer of gelatin mixture. Chill until firm.

Spicy Cranberry Salad

Cranberries are a must for Christmas!

1 (6 ounce) package raspberry gelatin
¼ teaspoon salt
½ teaspoon cinnamon
⅛ teaspoon cloves
1 cup boiling water
2 (16 ounce) cans whole cranberry sauce
1 (8 ounce) can crushed pineapple
1 (11 ounce) can mandarin oranges, drained

Place gelatin, salt, cinnamon and cloves in large mixing bowl and pour boiling water over gelatin. Mix until gelatin dissolves thoroughly.

Add both cans cranberry sauce, pineapple and oranges.

Pour into 9 x 13-inch dish sprayed with vegetable cooking spray and chill until firm.

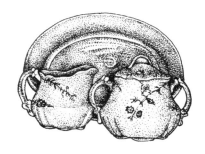

Apricot Salad

Apricots are an everyday treat!

1 (6 ounce) package apricot gelatin
¾ cup boiling water
1 (8 ounce) package cream cheese, softened
2 tablespoons sugar
¾ cup chopped pecans
1 (8 ounce) can crushed pineapple with juice
1 (16 ounce) can apricots, drained
1 (8 ounce) carton whipped topping

In mixing bowl, mix gelatin with boiling water until gelatin dissolves.

Add cream cheese and beat until fairly smooth. Stir in sugar, pecans and pineapple.

Cut each apricot half into fourths. Fold apricots and whipped topping into gelatin mixture.

Pour into 9 x 13-inch glass dish and chill.

Yuletide Salad

Red and green are special for Christmas.

1 (6 ounce) package red raspberry gelatin
1 cup boiling water
1 (20 ounce) can cherry pie filling
1 (8 ounce) can crushed pineapple with juice
¾ cup chopped pecans
1 (6 ounce) package lime gelatin
¾ cup boiling water
1 (8 ounce) package cream cheese, softened
1 (8 ounce) can crushed pineapple with juice
¾ (8 ounce) carton whipped topping
4 or 5 drops green food coloring

Dissolve raspberry gelatin in boiling water.

Add cherry pie filling, pineapple and pecans. Pour into 9 x 13-inch glass dish sprayed with vegetable cooking spray and chill until partially set.

In mixing bowl, dissolve lime gelatin in ¾ cup boiling water and mix well.

Add cream cheese and whip (slowly at first) until cream cheese melts. Add pineapple and chill in refrigerator.

When green mixture thickens, fold in whipped topping and green food coloring. Spread over top of raspberry mixture and chill.

Cranapple Wiggle

A family friend made this recipe a tradition.

1 (6 ounce) package cherry gelatin
1½ cups boiling water
1 (16 ounce) can whole cranberry sauce
1 (15 ounce) can crushed pineapple with juice
1 cup chopped apples
1 cup chopped pecans

Dissolve gelatin in boiling water and mix well.

Add cranberry sauce, pineapple, apples and pecans.

Pour into 9 x 13-inch glass dish sprayed with vegetable cooking spray and chill. Stir about the time it begins to set so the apples will not all stay on top.

Serves 12.

Cinnamon Salad

3 cups water
2 (6 ounce) packages cherry gelatin
⅔ cup cinnamon red hot candies
1 (25 ounce) jar applesauce
2 teaspoons lemon juice

Filling:
2 (8 ounce) packages cream cheese, softened
1 cup mayonnaise
1 cup chopped walnuts

In large saucepan, heat water to boiling, add gelatin and stir until it dissolves.

Lower heat to moderately low and add candies. Continue heating and stirring until candies dissolve. Remove from heat and add applesauce and lemon juice.

Pour half of gelatin mixture into 9 x 13-inch baking dish. Set aside remaining gelatin mixture at room temperature.

Place first layer in freezer for about 1 hour or until set.

In mixing bowl, combine cream cheese and mayonnaise until fairly smooth and mix in walnuts.

When first layer of gelatin is firmly set, spread cream cheese mixture over top. Chill about 30 minutes and pour remaining gelatin mixture over top. Chill several hours.

Serves 15.

Pink-Poinsettia Salad

This makes a pretty salad for a luncheon.

1 (6 ounce) package raspberry gelatin
1 cup boiling water
1 (20 ounce) can blueberry pie filling
1 (8 ounce) can crushed pineapple with juice
1 cup chopped pecans
1 (8 ounce) carton whipped topping

Dissolve gelatin in boiling water and stir well.

Stir in pie filling, crushed pineapple and pecans.

Set in refrigerator for about 30 minutes to chill.

When chilled, fold in whipped topping and pour into
9 x 13-inch glass dish sprayed with vegetable cooking spray.

When ready to serve, cut in squares and serve on lettuce leaf.

Serves 12.

Lime-Mint Salad

The buttermints make this recipe a special treat.

2 (16 ounce) cans crushed pineapple, drained
1 (6 ounce) package lime gelatin
1 (10 ounce) package tiny marshmallows
1 (12 ounce) carton whipped topping
1 teaspoon pineapple extract
½ teaspoon mint extract
1 (8 ounce) box buttermints, crushed

Mix pineapple, dry gelatin and marshmallows in bowl and set overnight at room temperature.

Next day fold in whipped topping, pineapple extract, mint extract and buttermints.

Pour into 9 x 13-inch glass dish and freeze.

Remove from freezer a few minutes before cutting and serving.

Serves 12.

Incredible Strawberry Salad

It really is incredible!

2 (8 ounce) packages cream cheese, softened
2 tablespoons mayonnaise
½ cup powdered sugar
1 (16 ounce) package frozen strawberries, thawed
1 cup small marshmallows
1 (8 ounce) can crushed pineapple, drained
1 (8 ounce) carton whipped topping
1 cup chopped pecans

In large mixing bowl, combine cream cheese, mayonnaise and powdered sugar and beat until creamy.

Fold in strawberries (if strawberries are large, cut them in half), marshmallows, pineapple, whipped topping and pecans.

Pour into 9 x 13-inch glass dish and freeze. Remove from freezer about 15 minutes before cutting and serving.

Serves 12.

Champagne Salad

This is a great salad to make ahead of time!

¾ cup powdered sugar
1 (8 ounce) package cream cheese, softened
1½ cups maraschino cherries, well drained, cut in half
1 (20 ounce) can crushed pineapple, drained
2 bananas, mashed
1 (8 ounce) carton whipped topping
1 cup chopped pecans
1½ cups miniature marshmallows

Cream sugar and cream cheese.

Fold in cherries, pineapple, bananas, whipped topping, pecans and marshmallows and mix well.

Pour into 9 x 13-inch pan sprayed with vegetable cooking spray and freeze.

Thaw 15 minutes before cutting in squares to serve.

Frozen Holiday Salad

2 (3 ounce) packages cream cheese, softened
3 tablespoons mayonnaise
¼ cup sugar
1 (16 ounce) can whole cranberry sauce
1 (8 ounce) can crushed pineapple, drained
1 cup chopped pecans
1 cup tiny marshmallows
1 (8 ounce) carton whipped topping

Mix cream cheese, mayonnaise and sugar.

Add fruit, pecans and marshmallows and fold in whipped topping.

Pour into greased 9 x 13-inch shallow glass dish and freeze.

When ready to serve, remove from freezer a few minutes before cutting into squares.

Creamy Gazpacho Salad

This is a great salad that is not sweet! A great discovery!

1 (10 ounce) can tomato soup
1 (3 ounce) envelope plain gelatin
¼ cup cold water
1 (8 ounce) package cream cheese, softened
½ cup chopped celery
½ cup chopped bell pepper
1 tablespoon finely chopped onion
1 teaspoon lemon juice
½ cup chopped pecans
1 cup mayonnaise
⅓ cup sliced green olives

Heat soup, gelatin and water on medium heat.

Add cream cheese, stirring constantly, blend well and chill.

Add remaining ingredients and pour mixture into mold or 9 x 9-inch glass dish and set overnight.

Cut into squares to serve.

Serves 8.

Tip: To make a main dish, add 1 cup cooked shrimp.

Cranberry-Chicken Salad

Layer 1:
1½ (3 ounce) envelopes unflavored gelatin
¼ cup cold water
1 (16 ounce) can whole cranberry sauce
1 (8 ounce) can crushed pineapple with juice
¼ cup sugar
1 cup chopped pecans
Red food coloring, optional

Layer 2:
1½ (3 ounce) envelopes unflavored gelatin
¼ cup cold water
½ cup water
1 (3 ounce) package cream cheese
3 tablespoons lemon juice
¾ teaspoon salt
2 cups diced cooked chicken
¾ cup chopped celery
¼ cup sweet relish
1 cup chopped pecans

Layer 1: Soften gelatin in cold water and set aside.

Place cranberry sauce, pineapple and sugar in saucepan and heat to boiling point.

Add gelatin mixture and stir well. Mix in pecans and red food coloring.

Pour into 9 x 13-inch glass dish sprayed with vegetable cooking spray and chill.

(continued on next page)

(continued)

Layer 2: Soften gelatin in ¼ cup cold water.

Place ½ cup water, cream cheese, lemon juice and salt in saucepan.

Bring to boil, stir until cream cheese dissolves and stir in gelatin mixture.

Fold in chicken, celery, relish and pecans. Pour on top of cranberry mixture and chill.

To serve, cut into squares and put cranberry side up on a bed of lettuce.

Cashew Salad

1 (6 ounce) package lemon gelatin
1 cup boiling water
1 quart vanilla ice cream
1 (15 ounce) can fruit cocktail, drained
1¼ cups cashew nuts

Dissolve gelatin in boiling water, add ice cream and stir until it melts.

Add fruit cocktail and cashew nuts and blend well.

Pour into 8 x 11-inch glass dish and chill overnight.

Artichoke Salad

1 (3 ounce) envelope plain gelatin
¼ cup cold water
½ cup boiling water
1 cup mayonnaise (not salad dressing)
1 (14 ounce) can artichoke hearts, well drained
½ (10 ounce) package frozen green peas, thawed, uncooked
2 tablespoons lemon juice
1 (4 ounce) jar chopped pimentos, drained
1 bunch green onions with tops, finely chopped
1½ cups shredded mozzarella cheese
1 teaspoon Italian herb seasoning
⅛ teaspoon cayenne pepper
⅛ teaspoon garlic powder
Paprika

Soften gelatin in cold water, add boiling water and mix well. Add mayonnaise and stir until smooth.

Remove any spikes or tough leaves from artichoke hearts and chop.

Add all remaining ingredients except paprika.

Pour into ring mold and chill.

When ready to serve, slip knife around edges to loosen from mold. Unmold onto serving plate lined with lettuce.

Sprinkle paprika over salad.

Tip: You could put radishes, olives or black olives, etc., in center of mold when serving.

Broccoli-Noodle Salad

*Very different, but very good and it will last
in the refrigerator for several days.*

1 cup slivered almonds, toasted
1 cup sunflower seeds, toasted
2 packages uncooked, chicken, Ramen noodles
1 (12 ounce) package broccoli slaw

Dressing:
¾ cup oil
½ cup white vinegar
½ cup sugar

Preheat oven to 275°. Toast almonds and sunflower seeds in
oven at 275° for about 15 minutes.

Break up Ramen noodles and mix with slaw, almonds and
sunflower seeds.

In separate bowl, mix dressing ingredients. Pour over slaw
mixture and mix well.

Make at least 1 hour before serving.

Tip: See page 172 for instructions to toast almonds.

Special Spinach Salad

1 (10 ounce) package fresh spinach
½ (14 ounce) can bean sprouts
1 (8 ounce) can water chestnuts, drained, sliced
3 hard-boiled eggs, sliced
1 bunch green onions with tops, chopped
6 strips bacon, crisply fried, crumbled

Dressing:
½ cup oil
½ cup white vinegar
⅓ cup sugar
2 tablespoons brown sugar
3 tablespoons ketchup
1 tablespoon Worcestershire
½ teaspoon salt

Wash spinach. (It must be dried very well. Shake several times in dry cup towel.) Remove stems from spinach and tear into small pieces.

In large bowl, combine spinach, bean sprouts, water chestnuts, eggs and onions and toss.

Add bacon just before serving.

Mix dressing and pour about ½ of dressing over salad. (It may be enough, but some may want more dressing.)

Cauliflower-Broccoli Salad

1 (8 ounce) carton sour cream
1 cup mayonnaise
1 (1 ounce) package original ranch dressing mix
1 large head cauliflower, broken in bite-size pieces
1 large bunch fresh broccoli, broken into bite-size pieces
1 (10 ounce) box frozen green peas, thawed, uncooked
3 ribs celery, sliced
1 bunch green onions with tops, chopped
1 (8 ounce) can water chestnuts, drained
⅓ cup sweet relish, drained
8 ounces mozzarella cheese, cubed
2 (2.25 ounce) packages slivered almonds, toasted

Mix sour cream, mayonnaise and dressing mix and set aside.

MAKE SURE cauliflower and broccoli are WELL DRAINED.

In a large container mix all salad ingredients.

Add dressing, toss and chill.

Serves 12.

Tip: See page 172 for instructions to toast almonds.

Caruso Salad

Pasta salad at its best!

½ pound curly vegetable pasta
1 small bunch broccoli, cut into bite-size pieces
2 small zucchini, sliced
½ red bell pepper, chopped
4 ounces pepperoni, cut into strips
8 ounces mozzarella cheese, cubed
1 (6 ounce) jar artichoke hearts, cut in pieces with juice
1 (8 ounce) jar Italian dressing

Cook pasta according to package directions. Rinse in cold water.

Toss with broccoli, zucchini, bell pepper, pepperoni and cheese and mix thoroughly.

Mix in artichoke hearts with oil in jar and toss with Italian dressing.

Cover and chill at least 2 hours before serving. Stir again before serving.

Serves 10 to 12.

Veggie Salad

Crunchy and good!

5 zucchini, sliced paper thin
4 yellow squash, sliced paper thin
1 head cauliflower, cut in bite-size pieces
1 red bell pepper, chopped
1 bunch green onions with tops, sliced
2 (2 ounce) packages slivered almonds, toasted
½ teaspoon salt
¼ teaspoon black pepper
1 (8 ounce) bottle creamy Italian dressing

Mix zucchini, yellow squash, cauliflower, bell pepper, onions, almonds, salt and pepper.

Add dressing and toss. Chill several hours before serving.

Tip: See page 172 for instructions to toast almonds.

Oriental Salad

1 (14 ounce) can Chinese vegetables
1 (10 ounce) package frozen Chinese pea pods cooked,
   halved
½ red bell pepper, sliced very thin
1 bunch green onions with tops, sliced
1 cup chopped celery
¾ cup slivered almonds, toasted
1 (8 ounce) can water chestnuts
1 package uncooked, Ramen noodles, broken

Dressing:
½ cup oil
¾ cup sugar
¾ cup white vinegar
½ teaspoon salt
1½ teaspoons seasoned pepper
½ teaspoon garlic powder
Flavor packet in Ramen noodles

Combine and mix all salad ingredients in large bowl.

For dressing, combine all ingredients and pour over salad and
toss.

Chill for several hours before serving.

Tip: See page 172 for instructions to toast almonds.

Broccoli Salad

The grapes give the recipe a special "zip".

1 large bunch broccoli, cut in bite-size pieces
1 cup chopped celery
1 bunch green onions with tops, sliced
½ red bell pepper, chopped
1 cup seedless green grapes, halved
1 cup seedless red grapes, halved
1 cup slivered almonds, toasted
½ pound bacon, cooked crisp, drained, crumbled

Dressing:
1 cup mayonnaise
¼ cup sugar
2 tablespoons vinegar
1 teaspoon salt
½ teaspoon black pepper

Wash and drain broccoli well. (It will help to drain broccoli if you will place pieces on a cup towel, pick it up and shake well.)

Mix all salad ingredients and toss.

Mix dressing ingredients and add to salad. Toss and refrigerate.

Serves 8 to 10.

Tip: See page 172 for instructions to toast almonds.

Cherry-Cranberry Salad

This is quick, easy and great!

1 (6 ounce) package cherry gelatin
1 cup boiling water
1 (20 ounce) can cherry pie filling
1 (16 ounce) can whole cranberry sauce

In mixing bowl, combine cherry gelatin and boiling water and mix until gelatin dissolves.

Add pie filling and cranberry sauce and mix well.

Pour into 7 x 11-inch dish and refrigerate. Serve on a lettuce leaf.

Serves 6 to 8.

Mincemeat Salad

1¾ cups orange juice
1 (6 ounce) package lemon gelatin
2 cups prepared mincemeat
1 cup chopped celery
1 cup chopped pecans
1 (15 ounce) can crushed pineapple, drained
1 medium apple, diced
1 tablespoon lemon juice

Heat orange juice, add gelatin, stir until it dissolves.

Stir in mincemeat, celery, pecans and pineapple.

Sprinkle lemon juice over apple and toss. Add to other ingredients.

Pour into 9 x 13-inch glass dish sprayed with vegetable cooking spray and chill.

Serves 12.

Creamy Fruit Salad

Choose your favorite pie filling for this salad.

1 (14 ounce) can sweetened condensed milk
¼ cup lemon juice
1 (20 ounce) can peach pie filling
1 (15 ounce) can pineapple chunks, drained
2 (15 ounce) cans fruit cocktail, drained
1 cup chopped pecans
1 (8 ounce) carton whipped topping

In large bowl, combine condensed milk and lemon juice and stir until well mixed.

Add pie filling, pineapple chunks, fruit cocktail and pecans, mix and fold in whipped topping.

Serve in a pretty crystal bowl.

Serves 12 to 14.

Holiday Turkey Dinner

Cranapple Wiggle, Page 68
Sweet Potato Casserole, Page 91
Turkey, Dressing and Gravy, Page 92
Almond-Asparagus Bake, Page 93
Colorful Party Peas, Page 94
Holiday Lemon-Pecan Cake With Whipped Cream, Page 116

CHOOSING YOUR TURKEY

To serve turkey for more than one meal, allow 1½ to 2 pounds per person. To serve for one meal only, allow ¾ to 1 pound per person if the turkey weighs less than 12 pounds. Allow ½ to ¾ pound per serving if turkey weighs over 12 pounds.

THAWING THE TURKEY

Place on a tray in refrigerator in original wrap. Allow 2 days for defrosting a turkey under 10 pounds. Allow 3 days for defrosting a 10 to 14-pound turkey. Allow 4 days for defrosting a 15 to 20-pound turkey. When ready to cook, remove metal clamp from legs. Run cold water into breast and neck cavities until giblets and neck can be removed. Interior should be cold to slightly icy. Chill until ready to cook.

CARVING THE TURKEY

Use a sharp carving knife, a two-tined meat fork and a serving plate for sliced meat.

Insert fork into drumstick joint, pulling the leg away from the body. Slice down until the ball and socket hip joint is exposed.

Make a twisting motion with the knife and continue to hold down firmly with the fork.

Cut joint as shown below:

Repeat the same for cutting off the other leg. Some slices of meat may be cut for those who prefer dark meat. Proceed to remove wings in a similar manner. To slice the breast, begin at area nearest the neck and slice thinly across the grain. Slice entire length of breast. Carve only one side until more is needed.

COOKING THE TURKEY

Preheat oven to 450°.

Rub entire turkey with butter and lightly salt (optional) and pepper all over. Place turkey in roaster, breast side up.

Cover bottom of pan with ½ to 1 cup water. Place 1 or 2 ribs celery and ½ peeled white onion inside cavity. Put lid on or cover loosely with foil.

Follow the cooking time chart and baste occasionally with drippings while turkey is cooking.

When ready to place turkey in the oven, turn heat to 325°.

Weight (pounds) of Unstuffed Turkey & Cooking time (hours) at 325°

WEIGHT	TIME	WEIGHT	TIME
6 to 8	3 to 3½	16 to 20	5½ to 6½
8 to 12	3½ to 4½	20 to 24	6½ to 7
12 to 16	4½ to 5½		

The turkey will be done when meat thermometer inserted in thigh registers 180 to 185° or breast temperature registers 170° to 175° and leg joint moves freely.

In the last 45 minutes of cooking time, remove lid and allow for final browning.

Sweet Potato Casserole

This is a terrific sweet potato dish.
Maybe it is time to graduate from marshmallows.

1 (29 ounce) can sweet potatoes, drained
⅓ cup evaporated milk
¾ cup sugar
2 eggs, beaten
¼ cup (½ stick) butter, melted
1 teaspoon vanilla

Topping:
1 cup packed light brown sugar
⅓ cup butter, melted
½ cup flour
1 cup chopped pecans

Preheat oven to 350°.

Place sweet potatoes in mixing bowl and mash slightly with fork.

Add evaporated milk, sugar, eggs, butter and vanilla and mix well.

Pour into greased 7 x 11-inch baking dish.

Mix topping ingredients and sprinkle over top of casserole.

Bake, uncovered, for 35 minutes or until crusty on top.

Serves 8.

Cornbread Dressing And Gravy

The best dressing in the world!

2 (6 ounce) packages cornbread mix
9 biscuits or 1 recipe of biscuit mix
1 small onion, chopped
2 ribs celery, chopped
2 eggs
Black pepper
2 teaspoons poultry seasoning
3 (14½ ounce) cans chicken broth, divided

Gravy:
2 (14 ounce) cans chicken broth
2 heaping tablespoons cornstarch
Black pepper
2 hard-boiled eggs, sliced, optional

Several days ahead of time prepare cornbread and biscuits according to package instructions.

Preheat oven to 350°.

Crumble cornbread and biscuits into large bowl, using a little more cornbread than biscuits.

Add onion, celery, eggs and seasonings. Stir in 2½ cans chicken broth. (If the mixture is not "runny", add remaining broth. If it is still not runny, add a little milk.)

Bake in 9 x 13-inch glass baking dish sprayed with vegetable cooking spray for about 45 minutes or until golden brown. This may be frozen uncooked, thawed and cooked when you want it.

(continued on next page)

(continued)

For gravy, mix cornstarch with ½ cup broth in saucepan and mix until there are no lumps.

Add remaining broth and heat to boiling, stirring constantly, until broth thickens.

Add hard-boiled eggs and pour into a gravy bowl.

Almond-Asparagus Bake

5 (10 ounce) cans asparagus
1½ cups cracker crumbs
4 eggs, hard-boiled, divided, sliced
1½ cups grated cheddar cheese
½ cup (1 stick) butter, melted
½ cup milk
2 (2.5 ounce) packages sliced almonds

Preheat oven to 350°.

Drain asparagus and arrange half asparagus in 9 x 13-inch baking dish sprayed with vegetable cooking spray.

Cover with ¾ cup crumbs and half sliced eggs and sprinkle with ½ cheese.

Layer remaining asparagus, ¾ cup crumbs and remaining eggs.

Drizzle butter and milk over casserole and top with almonds and remaining cheese.

Bake at 350° for 30 minutes.

Serves 10 to 12.

Colorful Party Peas

Delicious!

4 tablespoons water
1 (16 ounce) package frozen green peas
1 (6 ounce) jar sliced mushrooms, drained
1 (4 ounce) jar chopped pimentos, drained
¼ cup (½ stick) butter
1 (8 ounce) can water chestnuts, drained
1 tablespoon sugar
½ teaspoon salt
¼ teaspoon white pepper
3 tablespoons cornstarch
½ cup milk
1 (8 ounce) jar mild Mexican processed cheese spread

In large saucepan, combine water, peas, mushrooms, pimentos, butter, water chestnuts, sugar, salt and pepper.

Bring to a boil and let simmer 5 to 10 minutes.

In small bowl, mix cornstarch and milk and stir well. Pour into vegetables and stir.

Cook on low heat just until mixture thickens.

While on low heat, add cheese spread and stir just until cheese melts. Pour into serving bowl.

Serves 8 to 10.

*Holiday Ham
Dinner*

Holiday Ham Dinner

Creamy Mashed Potatoes, Page 95
Apricot-Baked Ham, Page 96
Cheesy Green Beans, Page 97
Baked Corn, Page 98
Winter Fruit Salad, Page 99
Cinnamon-Almond Pecan Pie, Page 131

You may choose to serve the glazed, spiral sliced ham at room temperature or heated.

To serve hot, preheat oven to 325° and place ham in shallow pan on rack uncovered. For whole ham, cook 15 minutes per pound. For a half ham, allow about 10 minutes per pound.

It would be delicious served with the Hot and Sweet Mustard Sauce on page 175.

Creamy Mashed Potatoes

6 large potatoes
1 (8 ounce) carton sour cream
1 (8 ounce) package cream cheese, softened
1 teaspoon salt
½ teaspoon white pepper

Preheat oven to 350°.

Peel, cut up, boil potatoes until fork tender and drain.

Whip hot potatoes, add sour cream, cream cheese, salt and pepper and whip until cream cheese melts.

Pour into greased 3-quart baking dish. Cover with foil and bake for about 20 minutes. (About 10 minutes longer if you are reheating them.)

Serves 8 to 10.

Tip: This may be made the day before serving and reheated.

Apricot-Baked Ham

1 (12 to 15 pound) whole ham, fully cooked, bone-in
Whole cloves
2 tablespoons dry mustard
1¼ cups apricot jam
1¼ cups packed light brown sugar

Preheat oven to 450°.

Trim skin and excess fat from ham. Place ham in large roasting pan.

Insert cloves in ham every inch or so. Be sure to push cloves into the ham surface as far as they will go.

Combine dry mustard and jam and spread over entire surface of ham. Pat brown sugar over jam mixture.

Reduce heat from 450° to 325° and bake uncovered for 15 minutes per pound.

The sugary crust that forms on the ham keeps the juices inside. When ham is done, remove from oven and let ham rest about 20 minutes before serving.

Tip: I usually buy a 10 to 12 pound "butt" end half ham. And this crusty recipe makes it delicious!

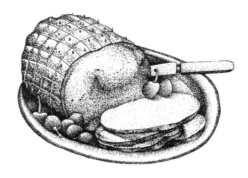

Cheesy Green Beans

3 (16 ounce) cans green beans, drained
1 (8 ounce) can sliced water chestnuts, drained
2 (8 ounce) jars processed cheese spread
1 cup cracker crumbs
2 (6 ounce) cans onion rings

Preheat oven to 350°.

Place green beans in greased 9 x 13-inch baking dish and cover with water chestnuts.

Heat both jars of cheese in microwave just until cheese can be poured. Pour cheese spread over green beans and water chestnuts.

Sprinkle cracker crumbs over cheese. Arrange onion rings over the casserole and bake at 350° for 30 minutes.

Serves 12.

Baked Corn

¼ cup (½ stick) butter
1 (8 ounce) package cream cheese
2 (16 ounce) packages frozen corn
1 (4 ounce) can chopped green chilies, drained
2 ribs celery, sliced
1 bell pepper, chopped
½ teaspoon seasoned salt
½ teaspoon white pepper
1½ cups crushed cracker crumbs

Preheat oven to 350°.

On low heat, melt butter in large saucepan, stir in cream cheese and stir until cream cheese melts.

Add corn, green chilies, celery, bell pepper, salt and pepper and mix well.

Pour into greased 9 x 13-inch baking dish. Sprinkle cracker crumbs over casserole.

Bake for 30 minutes.

Serves 10.

Winter Fruit Salad

2 (11 ounce) cans mandarin oranges
2 (15.5 ounce) cans pineapple chunks
1 (16 ounce) package frozen strawberries
1 (20 ounce) can peach pie filling
1 (20 ounce) can apricot pie filling
2 bananas, sliced

Drain oranges, pineapple and strawberries.

Combine all ingredients, fold salad gently so no fruit will be broken and chill.

Serves 12 to 15.

Tip: If you want to make a day early, mix oranges, pineapple and pie fillings and add drained strawberries and bananas at the last minute.

Jazzy Turkey And Dressing

1 (8 ounce) package stuffing
3 cups diced, cooked turkey
1 (15 ounce) can golden hominy, drained
1 (4 ounce) can chopped green chilies, drained
½ cup chopped red bell pepper
2 tablespoons dried parsley flakes
1 (10 ounce) can cream of chicken soup, undiluted
1 (8 ounce) carton sour cream
½ cup water
2 tablespoons (¼ stick) butter, melted
2 teaspoons ground cumin
½ teaspoon salt
1 cup shredded mozzarella cheese

Preheat oven to 350°.

In large mixing bowl, combine all ingredients except cheese and mix well.

Pour into greased 9 x 13-inch baking dish and cover with foil.

Bake at 350° for 35 minutes.

Uncover, sprinkle with cheese and bake an additional 5 minutes.

Serves 10 to 12.

Tortilla Delight

1 (9½ ounce) bag tortilla chips
1 onion, chopped
3 ribs celery, chopped
1 (10 ounce) can cream of chicken soup
2 (10 ounce) cans tomatoes and green chilies, drained
1 (1 pound) processed cheese, cubed
3½ cups cooked, diced turkey or chicken

Preheat oven to 350°.

Spray 9 x 13-inch baking dish with vegetable cooking spray and place half of bag of tortilla chips in dish. Crush a little with the palm of hand.

In large saucepan, combine onion, celery, chicken soup, tomatoes and green chilies and cheese over medium heat and stir until cheese melts.

Add turkey pieces and pour over tortilla chips.

Crush remaining tortilla chips in plastic bag with a rolling pin. Sprinkle over turkey-cheese mixture.

Bake at 350° for 35 minutes or until bubbly around edges.

Serves 8 to 10.

Divine Turkey Casserole

1 (16 ounce) package frozen broccoli spears
1 teaspoon seasoned salt
3 cups diced, cooked turkey or chicken
1 (10 ounce) can cream of chicken soup, undiluted
2 tablespoons milk
⅓ cup mayonnaise
2 teaspoons lemon juice
¼ teaspoon black pepper
3 tablespoons butter, melted
1 cup breadcrumbs or cracker crumbs
⅓ cup shredded cheddar cheese

Preheat oven to 350°.

Cook broccoli according to package directions and drain.

Place broccoli in 8 x 12-inch glass baking dish sprayed with vegetable cooking spray, sprinkle seasoned salt over top and cover with diced turkey.

In saucepan, combine soup, milk, mayonnaise, lemon juice and pepper. Heat just enough to dilute soup a little and pour over turkey.

Mix melted butter, breadcrumbs and cheese and sprinkle over soup mixture.

Bake uncovered at 350° for 30 minutes or until mixture is hot and bubbly.

Serves 6.

Creamy Turkey Enchiladas

2 tablespoons butter
1 onion, finely chopped
3 green onions with tops, chopped
½ teaspoon garlic powder
½ teaspoon seasoned salt
1 (7 ounce) can chopped green chilies, drained
2 (8 ounce) packages cream cheese, softened
3 cups diced turkey or chicken
8 (8 inch) flour tortillas
2 (8 ounce) cartons whipping cream
1 (16 ounce) package shredded Monterey Jack cheese

Preheat oven to 350°.

In large skillet, add butter and saute onions.

Add garlic powder, seasoned salt and green chilies and stir in cream cheese. Heat and stir until cream cheese melts and add diced turkey.

Lay out 8 tortillas and spoon about 3 heaping tablespoons turkey mixture on each tortilla.

Roll up tortillas and place seam side down in lightly greased 9 x 13-inch baking dish.

Pour whipping cream over enchiladas and sprinkle cheese over enchiladas.

Bake uncovered at 350° for 35 minutes.

Jalapeno Turkey

Even if you are not a spinach fan, you will like this recipe!

2 cups chopped onion
2 tablespoons butter
1 (10 ounce) package frozen spinach, cooked, drained
    thoroughly
6 jalapenos or 1 (7 ounce) can green chilies, drained
1 (8 ounce) carton sour cream
2 (10 ounce) cans cream of chicken soup
4 green onions with tops, chopped
½ teaspoon salt
1 (12 ounce) package tortilla chips, slightly crushed
4 cups diced turkey or chicken
1 (8 ounce) package shredded Monterey Jack cheese

Preheat oven to 350°.

Saute onion in butter. Blend in spinach, peppers, sour cream, soups, onion tops and salt.

In large 15 x 10-inch baking dish (or two 9 x 9-inch dishes), alternate tortilla chips, turkey, spinach mixture and cheese. Repeat layers with cheese on top.

Bake at 350° for 35 minutes.

Turkey And Ham Tetrazzini

1 (7 ounce) package spaghetti, cooked, drained
½ cup slivered almonds, toasted
1 (10 ounce) can cream of mushroom soup
1 (10 ounce) can cream of chicken soup
¾ cup milk
2 tablespoons dry white wine
2½ cups diced turkey
2 cups fully cooked, diced ham
½ cup chopped green bell pepper
½ cup halved pitted ripe olives
1 (8 ounce) package shredded cheddar cheese

Preheat oven to 350°.

Rinse cooked spaghetti with cold water to maintain firmness.

Mix almonds, soups, milk and wine in dish. Stir in spaghetti, turkey, ham, chopped pepper and pitted olives.

Pour into 9 x 13-inch baking dish sprayed with vegetable cooking spray. Sprinkle top of mixture with cheddar cheese.

Bake uncovered at 350° for 35 minutes or until hot and bubbly.

Serves 10.

Tip: See page 172 for instructions to toast almonds.

Spicy Turkey Soup

This is spicy, but not too much, just right!

3 to 4 cups chopped turkey
3 (10 ounce) cans condensed chicken broth, undiluted
2 (10 ounce) cans diced tomatoes and green chilies, drained
1 (16 ounce) can whole corn, drained
1 large onion, chopped
1 (10 ounce) can tomato soup
1 teaspoon garlic powder
1 teaspoon dried oregano
3 tablespoons cornstarch
3 tablespoons water

In large roaster, combine turkey, broth, tomatoes and green chilies, onion, corn, tomato soup, garlic powder and oregano.

Mix cornstarch with water and add to soup mixture.

Bring to boil, reduce heat and simmer, stirring occasionally, about 2 hours.

Yield about 2½ quarts.

Chinese Turkey

3½ cups cooked turkey, cut in bite-size pieces
2 (10 ounce) cans cream of chicken soup
1 (16 ounce) can chop suey vegetables, drained
1 (8 ounce) can sliced water chestnuts, drained
¾ cup cashew nuts
1 cup chopped green peppers
1 bunch green onions with tops, sliced
½ cup chopped celery
⅓ teaspoon hot sauce
¼ teaspoon curry powder
1 (5 ounce) can chow mein noodles

Preheat oven to 350°.

In large bowl, combine turkey, soups, vegetables, water chestnuts, cashew nuts, green pepper, green onions, celery, hot sauce and curry powder. Stir to mix well.

Spoon into 9 x 13-inch glass baking dish sprayed with vegetable cooking spray.

Sprinkle chow mein noodles over top of casserole.

Bake uncovered at 350° for 30 to 35 minutes or until bubbly at edges of casserole. Let sit 5 minutes before serving.

Serves 10.

Mexican-Turkey Fiesta

4 cups chopped turkey or 7 chicken breast halves, cooked
1 onion, chopped
1 (12 ounce) bag shredded cheddar cheese
1 green bell pepper, chopped
1 teaspoon chili powder
½ teaspoon salt
½ teaspoon black pepper
½ teaspoon ground cumin
2 (10 ounce) cans cream of chicken soup
1 (10 ounce) can diced green chilies and tomatoes, drained
1 (14 ounce) bag tortilla chips, divided

Preheat oven to 375°.

In large pan, combine all ingredients except tortilla chips and mix well.

Spray a 9 x 12-inch baking dish with vegetable cooking spray. Pour about two-thirds of tortilla chips into baking dish and crush slightly with palm of your hand.

Pour all turkey-cheese mixture over crushed tortilla chips and spread out.

Crush remaining tortilla chips in a baggie and spread over casserole.

Bake uncovered at 375° for 40 minutes.

Serves 12.

Three-Cheese Turkey Casserole

1 (8 ounce) package egg noodles
3 quarts water
1 tablespoon salt
1 teaspoon oil
3 tablespoons butter
¾ cup chopped green bell pepper
½ cup chopped celery
½ cup chopped onion
1 (10 ounce) can cream of chicken soup
½ cup milk
1 (6 ounce) jar whole mushrooms
½ teaspoon black pepper
1 (12 ounce) carton small-curd cottage cheese
4 cups diced turkey or chicken
1 (12 ounce) package shredded cheddar cheese
¾ cup freshly grated parmesan cheese

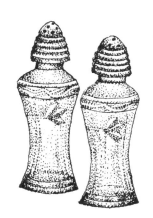

Preheat oven to 350°.

In large kettle, place noodles in hot water, add salt and oil and cook according to package directions.

Melt butter in skillet and saute bell pepper, celery and onion.

In large bowl, combine noodles, bell pepper-onion mixture, chicken soup, milk, mushrooms, black pepper, cottage cheese, turkey and cheddar cheese.

Pour into 9 x 13-inch baking dish sprayed with vegetable cooking spray. Top with parmesan cheese.

Bake uncovered at 350° for 40 minutes.

Serves 10.

Turkey Supreme

1 onion, chopped
1 cup sliced celery
3 tablespoons butter
4 cups diced, cooked turkey
1 (6 ounce) package long grain and wild rice, cooked
Seasoning packet in rice package
1 (10 ounce) can cream of celery soup
1 (10 ounce) can cream of chicken soup
1 (4 ounce) jar pimentos, drained
2 (15 ounce) cans French-style green beans, drained
1 cup slivered almonds
1 cup mayonnaise
½ teaspoon salt
1 teaspoon black pepper
2½ cups crushed potato chips

Preheat oven to 350°.

In large saucepan saute onion and celery in butter.

Add turkey, rice, seasoning packet, both soups, pimentos, green beans, almonds, mayonnaise and seasonings and stir.

Pour into greased 9 x 13-inch baking dish. (This needs a very large casserole dish.)

Sprinkle crushed potato chips over casserole.

Bake uncovered at 350° for 35 minutes or until potato chips brown slightly.

Tip: If you want to make in advance and freeze, add potato chips when ready to cook casserole.

Ham Chowder

*This is a real "tasty" way to use left-over ham
and it has a great flavor!*

1 cup sliced celery
½ cup chopped onion
2 tablespoons butter
3 cups shredded cabbage
3½ cups fully cooked diced ham
2 (16 ounce) cans Mexican-style stewed tomatoes with liquid
1 (15 ounce) can whole kernel corn, drained
1 (15 ounce) can whole potatoes, drained, sliced
1 (14 ounce) can condensed chicken broth, undiluted
1 cup water
½ cup ketchup
¼ cup packed light brown sugar
½ teaspoon salt
½ teaspoon garlic powder

In large roasting pan or soup kettle over medium heat, saute celery and onion in butter.

Add remaining ingredients and bring to boil.

Reduce heat, cover and simmer for 1 hour.

Pancho Villa Stew

3 cups diced, cooked ham
1 pound smoked kielbasa sausage, cut in ½-inch slices
3 (14 ounce) cans chicken broth
1 (15 ounce) can whole tomatoes with liquid
3 (4 ounce) cans chopped green chilies with liquid
1 large onion, chopped
1 teaspoon garlic powder
2 teaspoons ground cumin
2 teaspoons cocoa
1 teaspoon dried oregano
½ teaspoon salt
2 (15 ounce) cans pinto beans with liquid
1 (15 ounce) can hominy with liquid
1 (8 ounce) can whole kernel corn with liquid
Flour tortillas

In roasting pan combine ham, sausage, chicken broth, tomatoes, green chilies, onion, garlic powder, cumin, cocoa, oregano and salt.

Bring to boil, reduce heat and simmer 45 minutes.

Add pinto beans, hominy and corn and bring to boil.

Reduce heat and simmer another 15 minutes.

Tip: Serve with buttered flour tortillas or cornbread. They are both good with this recipe.

Crunchy Ham Salad

1 cup grated carrots
¾ cup finely chopped celery
¼ cup finely chopped onion
⅓ cup mayonnaise
1 teaspoon prepared mustard
⅓ cup sweet relish
⅛ teaspoon cayenne pepper, optional
½ teaspoon black pepper
1½ cups finely diced fully cooked ham
1 (1.5 ounce) can shoestring potato sticks

Combine carrots, celery, onion, mayonnaise, mustard, relish, cayenne pepper, black pepper and ham and toss. (Add a little more mayonnaise if salad seems to dry.)

Just before serving, add shoestring potatoes and toss.

Serves 8.

Tip: *Instead of prepared mustard, use 2 teaspoons Hot and Sweet Mustard on page 175. It adds a real zip to this salad.*

Raisin Sauce For Ham

1½ cups water
½ teaspoon ground cloves
1 cup packed brown sugar
1 tablespoon cornstarch
¼ teaspoon salt
1 cup raisins
1 tablespoon butter
1 tablespoon vinegar
¼ teaspoon Worcestershire

In saucepan, combine water, ground cloves, brown sugar, cornstarch and salt and mix well.

Add raisins, butter, vinegar and Worcestershire.

On medium heat, bring mixture close to boiling point, quickly reduce heat and simmer 10 to 15 minutes.

Serve over ham.

Cherry Sauce For Ham

1 (16 once) can pitted red tart cherries with liquid
¼ cup red wine
½ cup sugar
2 tablespoons cornstarch
1 tablespoon lemon juice
¼ teaspoon cinnamon

Drain cherry juice into saucepan and combine cherry juice, wine, sugar, cornstarch, lemon juice and cinnamon.

Cook over medium heat, stirring constantly, until mixture thickens.

Add cherries and heat. Serve over ham.

Holiday Lemon-Pecan Cake

This cake is delicious the day you make it and still better after several days! Try it and you will want it every Christmas!

1 (1.5 ounce) bottle lemon extract
4 cups pecan halves
2 cups (4 sticks) butter
3 cups sugar
3½ cups flour, divided
1½ teaspoons baking powder
6 eggs, divided
½ pound candied green pineapple, chopped
½ pound candied red cherries, halved

Preheat oven to 275°. Grease and flour a tube cake pan.

Pour lemon extract over pecans in medium bowl, toss and set aside.

In large mixing bowl, cream butter and sugar until fluffy.

Sift 3 cups flour and baking powder in separate bowl.

Add eggs to butter-sugar mixture, one at a time, alternately with flour mixture.

With pineapple and cherries cut, add ½ cup flour and mix so that flour covers fruit.

Fold in fruit and pecans and pour into tube pan.

Bake at 275° for 2 hours and 30 minutes to 2 hours and 45 minutes. Test after 2½ hours for doneness. Cool and remove carefully from pan.

Chocolate Hurricane Cake

*This is a light, chocolate delight that is delicious
and very easy to make!*

1 cup chopped pecans
1 (3.5 ounce) can sweetened flaked coconut
1 (18 ounce) box German chocolate cake mix
1¼ cups water
⅓ cup oil
3 eggs
½ cup (1 stick) butter, melted
1 (8 ounce) package cream cheese, softened
1 (1 pound) box powdered sugar

Preheat oven to 350°.

Grease and flour 9 x 13-inch baking pan. Cover bottom of pan
with pecans and coconut.

In mixing bowl, mix cake mix, water, oil and eggs and beat well.
Pour batter carefully over pecans and coconut.

In mixing bowl, combine butter, cream cheese and powdered
sugar and whip to blend. Spoon over unbaked batter.

Bake at 350° for 40 to 42 minutes. You cannot test for
doneness with cake tester because the cake will appear sticky
even when it is done.

*The icing sinks to the bottom as it bakes, forming the white
ribbon inside.*

Sweet Angel Cake

This is a super dessert you will want winter and summer!

1½ cups powdered sugar
⅓ cup milk
1 (8 ounce) package cream cheese, softened
1 (3½ ounce) can flaked coconut
1 cup chopped pecans
1 (12 ounce) carton whipped topping
1 large angel food cake, torn into bite-size pieces
1 (16 ounce) can cherry pie filling

Add sugar and milk to cream cheese and beat in mixing bowl.

Fold in coconut and pecans and stir in whipped topping and cake pieces. Spread in large 9 x 13-inch glass dish. Chill several hours.

Add pie filling by the tablespoon on top of the cake mixture. It will not cover the cake mixture, but it will just be in clumps, making a pretty red and white dessert. Chill.

Serves 15 to 16.

Apple-Date-Pecan Cake

This cake is so moist and just full of goodies!

2 cups sugar
1½ cups oil
3 eggs
2 teaspoons vanilla
2½ cups flour
1 teaspoon baking soda
½ teaspoon salt
1½ teaspoons cinnamon
¼ teaspoon ground ginger
3 cups chopped apples
1 (8 ounce) package chopped dates
1 cup chopped pecans

Glaze:
1 cup sugar
⅓ cup water
1 teaspoon almond extract

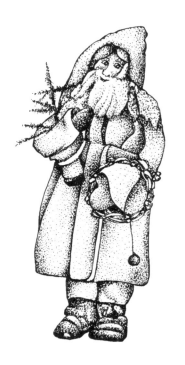

Preheat oven to 325°.

Blend sugar, oil, eggs and vanilla and beat well.

Add flour, baking soda, salt, cinnamon and ginger and beat well.

Fold in apples, dates, and pecans and pour into 10-inch greased, floured tube pan.

Bake at 325° for 1 hour and 30 minutes or until cake tests done.

Right before cake is done, bring sugar and water to rolling boil. Remove from heat and add almond extract.

Pour glaze over hot cake while still in pan. Let stand about 20 minutes before removing from pan.

Pumpkin Pie Pound Cake

*How could you miss with pumpkin pie
and pound cake all rolled up in one recipe!*

1 cup shortening
1¼ cups sugar
¾ cup packed brown sugar
5 eggs, room temperature
1 cup canned pumpkin
2½ cups flour
2 teaspoons cinnamon
1 teaspoon ground nutmeg
½ teaspoon mace
½ teaspoon salt
1 teaspoon baking soda
½ cup orange juice, room temperature
2 teaspoons vanilla
1½ cups chopped pecans

Icing:
2 cups powdered sugar
6 tablespoons (¾ stick) butter, melted
3 tablespoons orange juice
¼ teaspoon orange extract

Preheat oven to 325°.

Cream shortening and both sugars for about 5 minutes.

Add eggs, one at a time, and mix well after each addition.
Blend in the pumpkin.

(continued on next page)

Cakes

(continued)

In separate bowl, combine flour, spices, salt and baking soda and mix well.

Gradually beat dry ingredients into batter until well mixed. Fold in orange juice, vanilla and chopped pecans.

Pour into greased and floured bundt pan.

Bake at 325° for 1 hour and 5 to 10 minutes or until a tester comes out clean. Allow cake to rest in pan for 10 to 15 minutes and turn cake out onto rack to cool completely before icing.

For icing, thoroughly mix all icing ingredients and put on cooled cake.

Favorite Cake

1 butter pecan cake mix
1 cup almond toffee bits
1 cup chopped pecans
Powdered sugar

Preheat oven to 350°.

Mix cake mix according to package directions. Fold in toffee bits and pecans.

Pour into a greased and floured bundt cake pan.

Bake for 45 minutes or until toothpick inserted in center comes out clean.

Allow cake to cool several minutes; then remove cake from pan. Dust with sifted powdered sugar.

Surprise Cake

5 tablespoons butter, softened
1 (18 ounce) package dry, coconut-pecan frosting mix
1 cup uncooked oats
1 cup sour cream
4 eggs
1½ cups bananas, mashed
1 (18 ounce) box yellow cake mix

Preheat oven to 350°.

In saucepan, melt butter, stir in frosting mix and rolled oats until crumbly and set aside.

In large bowl, blend sour cream, eggs and bananas until smooth.

Fold in cake mix and beat 2 minutes.

Pour 2 cups batter into greased and floured tube pan. Sprinkle with 1 cup crumb mixture. Repeat twice with batter and crumbs, ending with crumb mixture.

Bake at 350° for 55 to 60 minutes. Cool in pan for 15 minutes.

Remove from pan and turn cake so crumb mixture is on top.

Pumpkin Cake

3 eggs
2 cups sugar
1 (15 ounce) can pumpkin
1 cup oil
2 cups flour
1 teaspoon baking soda
2 teaspoons baking powder
2 teaspoons cinnamon
½ teaspoon ginger
½ teaspoon cloves
½ teaspoon nutmeg
½ teaspoon salt

Frosting:
1 (3 ounce) package cream cheese, softened
6 tablespoons (¾ stick) butter, melted
3 cups powdered sugar
1 teaspoon vanilla
1 tablespoon milk

Preheat oven to 350°.

In mixing bowl, beat eggs, sugar, pumpkin and oil.

Add flour, baking soda, baking powder, spices and salt and mix well.

Pour into 9 x 13-inch greased and floured baking pan.

Bake at 350° for 30 to 35 minutes. Test for doneness.

Mix together all frosting ingredients. (Add more milk if frosting is too stiff.) Pour over hot cake.

Orange-Date Cake

4 cups flour
1 teaspoon baking soda
1 cup (2 sticks) butter, softened
2½ cups sugar
4 eggs
1½ cups buttermilk
1 teaspoon orange extract
1 tablespoon grated orange rind
1 (11 ounce) can mandarin oranges
1 (8 ounce) package pre-chopped dates
1 cup chopped pecans

Glaze:
½ cup orange juice
1¼ cups sugar
1 teaspoon orange rind
½ teaspoon orange extract

Preheat oven to 350°.

Sift flour and baking soda together and set aside.

Cream butter and sugar. Add eggs, one at a time, and beat well after each addition.

Add buttermilk and dry ingredients, alternately, ending with dry ingredients.

Add orange extract and rind and beat well. Stir in oranges, dates and pecans.

(continued on next page)

(continued)

Pour into greased and floured bundt pan and bake at 350° for 1 hour and 15 minutes or until cake tests done.

Remove from oven and pour glaze over cake while still in pan.

To make glaze, mix orange juice, sugar, orange rind and orange extract in saucepan and bring to boil and cool.

Tip: *This is so moist and good. If you don't happen to have buttermilk on hand, just put about 2 tablespoons lemon juice in 1½ cups milk and let it sit 10 or 15 minutes – presto, you'll have buttermilk.*

Cranberry-Almond Cake

This is good for dessert or as a coffee cake for breakfast.

½ cup (1 stick) butter, softened
1 cup sugar
2 eggs
1 teaspoon almond extract
2 cups flour
1 teaspoon baking powder
¼ teaspoon salt
1 (8 ounce) carton sour cream
1 cup whole cranberry sauce
¾ cup slivered almonds, chopped

Glaze:
1½ cups powdered sugar
2 tablespoons milk
½ teaspoon almond extract

Preheat oven to 350°.

Cream butter and sugar and beat until fluffy. Add eggs, beat after each addition and add almond extract.

Combine flour, baking powder and salt. Add flour mixture and sour cream, alternately to sugar mixture, beginning and ending with flour mixture.

Fold in cranberry sauce and almonds. Pour batter into greased and floured 9 x 13-inch baking pan.

Bake at 350° for 30 to 35 minutes or until cake tester comes out clean.

Combine glaze ingredients and drizzle over warm cake.

Brown Sugar-Rum Pound Cake

1½ cups (3 sticks) butter, softened
1 (16 ounce) package brown sugar
1 cup sugar
5 large eggs
¾ cup milk
¼ cup rum
2 teaspoons vanilla
3 cups flour
2 teaspoons baking powder
¼ teaspoon salt
1½ cups chopped pecans

Preheat oven to 325°.

With electric mixer, beat butter and both sugars at medium speed about 5 minutes. Add eggs, one at a time, and beat just until yellow disappears.

Combine milk, rum and vanilla in separate bowl. Combine flour, baking powder and salt in separate bowl.

Add half flour mixture to butter and sugar and mix. Add milk mixture and mix. Add remaining flour mixture and beat at low speed.

Fold in pecans and pour into greased and floured tube pan.

Bake at 325° for 1 hour and 25 minutes. Test with a toothpick to make sure cake is done.

Cool in pan for 20 minutes, remove from pan and cool.

Tip: If you don't want to use rum, just add ¼ cup milk and 2 teaspoons rum flavoring.

Red Velvet Pound Cake

*So pretty and kids love it! The icing and color
make this an extra special pound cake.*

3 cups sugar
¾ cup shortening
6 eggs
1 teaspoon vanilla
¼ teaspoon salt
3 cups flour
1 cup milk
2 (1 ounce) bottles red food coloring

Icing:
1 (1 pound) box powdered sugar
1 (3 ounce) package cream cheese, softened
¼ cup (½ stick) butter, softened
3 tablespoons milk
Red sprinkles

Preheat oven to 325°.

Cream sugar and shortening. Add eggs, one at a time, and beat
after each addition. Add vanilla and mix.

Add salt, flour and milk, alternately beginning and ending with
flour. Add food coloring and beat until smooth.

Bake in greased and floured tube pan at 325° for 1 hour and
30 minutes or until cake tests done. Let cake rest in pan for 10
minutes. Take cake out of pan and cool completely.

To make icing, cream powdered sugar, cream cheese, butter
and milk and mix well. Ice cake and top with a few red
sprinkles over white icing.

Angel Dust Pie

A favorite at our "testing" party!

3 egg whites
1 cup round, buttery cracker crumbs
Pinch of salt
1¼ cups sugar
2 teaspoons vanilla, divided
¾ cup chopped pecans
1 cup whipping cream
¼ cup powdered sugar
1 cube white chocolate, grated (white almond bark)

Preheat oven to 325°.

Beat egg whites to very stiff peaks. Combine cracker crumbs, salt, sugar, 1 teaspoon vanilla and pecans.

Fold into beaten egg whites and spread in buttered and floured 9-inch pie plate.

Bake at 325° for 45 minutes and cool completely.

Whip cream with powdered sugar and 1 teaspoon vanilla and spread over crust.

Sprinkle grated white chocolate over whipped cream and chill.

Holiday Fruit Pie

1 (16 ounce) can tart red cherries, drained, reserve juice
1 (15 ounce) can crushed pineapple, drained, reserve juice
Water
8 tablespoons cornstarch
2½ cups sugar
½ teaspoon salt
3 teaspoons red food coloring
1 cup chopped pecans
2 bananas, mashed
2 (9-inch) graham cracker pie crusts
1 (8 ounce) carton whipped topping

Add enough water to fruit juice to make 2 cups. Add fruit to juice.

Mix cornstarch and sugar and add to fruit along with salt and food coloring. (Add more red coloring if the fruit isn't very red.)

Cook until thick, stirring constantly, and cool.

Add pecans and bananas. Pour into 2 pie crusts. Divide whipped topping and spread on both pies.

Tip: This pie is better the day or day after it is made. If you don't need both pies, freeze one.

Cinnamon-Almond Pecan Pie

A little change from the traditional pecan pie, but a good one!

⅔ cup sugar
1 tablespoon flour
2½ teaspoons cinnamon
4 eggs, lightly beaten
1 cup light corn syrup
2 tablespoons butter, melted
1 tablespoon vanilla
1½ teaspoons almond extract
1 cup coarsely chopped pecans
½ cup slivered almonds
1 (9-inch) unbaked pie shell

Preheat oven to 400°.

In large bowl combine sugar and flour. Add cinnamon, eggs, corn syrup, butter, vanilla and almond extract and mix well.

Stir in chopped pecans and slivered almonds. Pour filling into pie shell.

Tear off 3 (1½-inch) strips of foil and cover crust (crimp a little where foil pieces come together) so it will not get too brown.

Bake at 400° for 10 minutes, reduce heat to 325° and bake 40 to 45 minutes more or until pie will just barely shake in center.

Cool completely before serving.

Almond-Mocha Pie

3 (1.55 ounce) chocolate bars
3 teaspoons instant coffee
1½ cups miniature marshmallows
½ cup milk
¼ cup amaretto liqueur
1 cup whipping cream, whipped
¼ cup powdered sugar
1 (9-inch) graham cracker pie crust
⅓ cup finely chopped almonds, toasted

Break candy bars in pieces and combine chocolate, instant coffee, marshmallows and milk in 1-quart glass bowl.

Microwave on 70% for 3 to 4 minutes, stirring after 2 minutes to see if it is necessary to microwave 1 or 2 more minutes. Mix until smooth, cool completely and stir in liqueur.

Chill in refrigerator until it begins to thicken.

Add powdered sugar to whipped cream and fold into marshmallow mixture. Pour into pie shell.

Garnish with toasted almonds and freeze. This pie can be cut easily right out of freezer.

Tip: See page 172 for instructions to toast almonds.

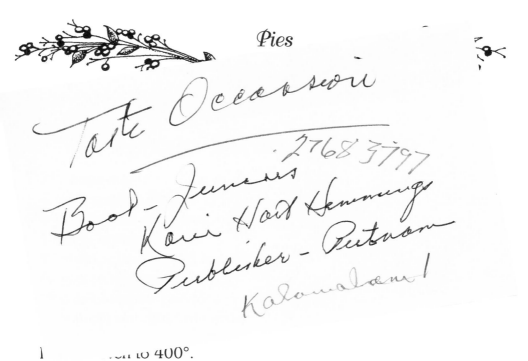

1   ...on to 400°.

Combine sugar, flour and cornmeal in large bowl and toss lightly.

Add eggs, lemon rind and lemon juice and mix until smooth and thoroughly blended.

Add pecans to mixture and pour into pie crust.

Tear off 3 (1½-inch) strips of foil and cover crust (crimp a little where foil pieces come together) so crust will not get too brown.

Bake at 400° for 10 minutes. Reduce oven temperature to 325° and bake 40 to 45 minutes or until center is not shaky.

Kahula-Pecan Pie

2 tablespoons butter, melted
1 cup sugar
1 teaspoon vanilla
3 tablespoons flour
3 eggs
⅓ cup kahula
½ cup white corn syrup
1 cup chopped pecans
1 (9-inch) unbaked pie shell

Preheat oven to 400°.

Melt butter in large bowl, add sugar, vanilla and flour and mix well.

Add eggs and beat a few minutes by hand. Pour in kahlua and corn syrup and mix.

Place pecans in pie shell and pour sugar-egg mixture over pecans.

Tear off 3 (1½-inch) strips of foil and cover crust (crimp a little where foil pieces come together) so crust will not get too brown.

Bake at 400° for 10 minutes, reduce heat to 325° and bake 40 to 45 minutes more or until pie will just barely shake in center.

Cool completely before serving.

Pumpkin-Chiffon Pie

1 (1 ounce) packet gelatin
¼ cup cold water
3 eggs
1 cup sugar, divided
1¼ cups canned pumpkin
⅔ cup milk
½ teaspoon ginger
½ teaspoon nutmeg
½ teaspoon cinnamon
½ teaspoon salt
1 (9-inch) baked pie crust

Soften gelatin in cold water and set aside.

Separate eggs and set whites aside. Beat yolks slightly and add ½ cup sugar, pumpkin, milk, spices and salt.

Cook in double boiler until custard consistency, stirring constantly.

Mix in softened gelatin, dissolve in hot custard and cool.

Beat egg whites and gradually add remaining sugar.

Fold stiffly beaten egg whites into cooled pumpkin mixture. Turn into cooked pie crust.

Chill several hours before slicing.

Pistachio-Lime Pie

A bridge club favorite!

2 cups vanilla wafer crumbs
¼ cup chopped pistachio nuts or pecans
¼ cup butter, melted
1 (8 ounce) package cream cheese, softened
1 (14 ounce) can sweetened condensed milk
¼ cup lime juice from concentrate
1 (3 ounce) package instant pistachio pudding mix
½ cup chopped pistachio nuts or pecans
1 (8 ounce) can crushed pineapple with juice
1 (8 ounce) carton whipped topping

Preheat oven to 350°.

Combine crumbs, ¼ cup nuts and butter and press firmly on bottom of 9-inch springform pan.

Bake at 350° for 8 to 10 minutes and cool.

In large mixing bowl, beat cream cheese until fluffy, gradually beat in sweetened condensed milk, then lime juice and pudding mix and beat until smooth.

Stir in ½ cup nuts and pineapple and fold in whipped topping.

Pour into springform pan and chill overnight. Keep chilled.

Apricot Cobbler

Everyone in the bridge club gave this a "blue ribbon".

1 (20 ounce) can apricot filling
1 (20 ounce) can crushed pineapple with juice
1 cup chopped pecans
1 (18 ounce) yellow cake mix
1 cup (2 sticks) butter, melted
Whipped topping

Preheat oven to 375°.

Spray 9 x 13-inch baking dish with vegetable cooking spray.

Pour apricot pie filling in pan and spread out.

Spoon crushed pineapple and juice over pie filling. Sprinkle pecans over pineapple, then sprinkle cake mix over pecans.

Pour melted butter over cake mix and bake at 375° for 40 minutes or until lightly brown and crunchy.

To serve, top with whipped topping.

Serves 10.

White Chocolate Pie

4 ounces white chocolate (white almond bark)
28 large marshmallows
½ cup milk
1 (8 ounce) carton whipped topping
½ cup chopped pecans
1 cup maraschino cherries, chopped, well drained
1 (9-inch) pie shell, baked

In double boiler melt white chocolate, marshmallows and milk and cool.

To cooled white chocolate mixture, add whipped topping, pecans and cherries.

Pour into pie shell and freeze. Remove from freezer 5 to 10 minutes before serving.

Creamy Lemon Pie

Lemony and creamy – a good combination!

1 (8 ounce) package cream cheese, softened
1 (14 ounce) can sweetened condensed milk
¼ cup lemon juice
1 (20 ounce) can lemon pie filling
1 (9-inch) graham cracker pie crust

In mixing bowl blend cream cheese until creamy.

Add sweetened condensed milk and lemon juice and beat until mixture is very creamy.

Fold in lemon pie filling, stir well and pour into pie crust.

Chill several hours before slicing and serving.

Date-Pecan Tarts

This is an old-time favorite!

1 (8 ounce) package chopped dates
2½ cups milk
½ cup flour
1½ cups sugar
3 eggs
½ teaspoon salt
1 teaspoon vanilla
1 cup chopped pecans
8 tart shells, baked, cooled
1 (8 ounce) carton whipping cream
3 tablespoons powdered sugar

In saucepan, cook dates, milk, flour and sugar until thick and stir constantly.

Add beaten eggs and salt and cook mixture about 5 minutes on medium heat and stir constantly.

Stir in vanilla and pecans, pour into tart shells and cool.

Whip whipping cream with powdered sugar and spread over top.

Strawberry Fluff

This is one of the lightest, fluffiest, most delicious desserts
you will ever eat! I talked a good friend out of this recipe.

1 cup (2 sticks) butter, softened
½ cup packed brown sugar
2 cups flour
1½ cups chopped pecans
2 egg whites
1 tablespoon lemon juice
1 cup sugar
2 (10 ounce) packages sweetened strawberries, thawed
1 tablespoon vanilla
1 (12 ounce) carton whipped topping

Preheat oven to 350°.

Combine and mix butter, brown sugar and flour until crumbly.
Add pecans and spread on cookie sheet.

Bake at 350° for about 15 minutes.

Spread this crumbly mixture in large 9 x 13-inch glass casserole
dish and cool.

In mixing bowl, beat egg whites for 5 minutes, add lemon juice,
1 cup sugar and both packages of strawberries and beat another
15 minutes.

This mixture will grow and grow and grow! Fold in whipped
topping, pour over crumbly crust mixture and freeze.

Reindeer Rapture

¾ cup packed brown sugar
¾ cup white sugar
1½ cups shortening
2 large eggs
1½ cups flour
½ teaspoon baking soda
½ teaspoon salt
2¾ cups oats
½ cup chopped pecans
½ cup peanut butter
1½ teaspoons vanilla
1 (6 ounce) package chocolate chips

Preheat oven to 350°.

Cream both sugars and shortening. Add eggs and beat.

Sift together flour, baking soda and salt. Add to creamed mixture and stir in oats, pecans, peanut butter, vanilla and chocolate chips.

Drop by teaspoonsful on cookie sheet.

Bake at 350° for 12 to 14 minutes or until cookies begin to brown on the edge.

Snappy Oats

*"Snappy" because you can make these
and not even heat up the oven.*

3 cups quick-rolled oats
1 cup chocolate chips or white chocolate chips
½ cup flaked coconut
½ cup chopped pecans
2 cups sugar
¾ cup (1½ sticks) butter
½ cup evaporated milk
¾ cup candied cherries, optional

Mix oats, chocolate chips, coconut and pecans in large bowl.

Bring sugar, butter and milk to rapid boil, boil 1½ minutes and
stir constantly.

Pour hot mixture over oats mixture and stir until chocolate chips
melt.

Drop by teaspoon on wax paper. Cool at room temperature
and store in covered container.

Mincemeat Cookies

For you "baby boomers" who don't know how good mincemeat is, don't overlook this recipe – it's great!

1 cup (2 sticks) butter, softened
1⅔ cups sugar
3 eggs, beaten
1 teaspoon baking soda
2 teaspoons hot water
½ teaspoon salt
3¼ cups flour
1¼ cups chopped pecans
1 cup prepared mincemeat

Preheat oven to 350°. Grease cookie sheets.

Cream butter and add sugar gradually.

Add eggs and baking soda dissolved in water and mix.

Add salt and flour to creamed mixture and mix well. Add pecans and mincemeat.

Drop by teaspoon on cookie sheets.

Bake at 350° for 14 to 15 minutes or until cookies begin to brown.

Cherry-Pecan Slices

A cherry lover's delight!

2 cups powdered sugar
1 cup (2 sticks) butter, softened
1 egg
2 tablespoons milk
1 teaspoon vanilla
2¼ cups flour
2 cups whole candied red cherries
1 cup chopped pecans

In mixing bowl, cream sugar and butter until slightly fluffy. Add egg, milk and vanilla, mix and beat in flour. Batter will be stiff.

Stir in cherries and pecans and mix well. Chill dough 1 hour.

Sprinkle a tiny bit of flour on wax paper. Shape dough into 2 (10-inch) rolls and wrap in wax paper. Chill at least 3 hours or overnight.

Preheat oven to 375°. Cut rolls into ¼-inch slices. Place on ungreased cookie sheets.

Bake at 375° for 10 to 12 minutes. Check cookies in 10 minutes; edges should be slightly brown.

Cool on wire racks and store in covered container.

Macadamia-Nut Cookies

Just like those good cookies you buy at the mall.

½ cup shortening
½ cup (1 stick) butter, softened
2½ cups flour, divided
1 cup packed brown sugar
½ cup granulated sugar
2 eggs
1 teaspoon vanilla
½ teaspoon butter flavoring
½ teaspoon baking soda
2 cups white chocolate chips
1 (3½ ounce) jar macadamia nuts, chopped

Preheat oven to 350°.

In mixing bowl, beat shortening and butter. Add half flour and mix well.

Add brown sugar, granulated sugar, eggs, vanilla, butter flavoring and baking soda and beat until mixture is well combined.

Add remaining flour, mix well and stir in chocolate pieces and nuts.

Drop dough by teaspoon onto ungreased cookie sheet.

Bake at 350° for about 8 minutes.

Dreamy Date Balls

½ cup (1 stick) butter
1 cup sugar
1 (8 ounce) box chopped dates
1 cup crispy rice cereal
1 cup chopped pecans
1 teaspoon vanilla
Powdered sugar

In large saucepan, combine butter, sugar and chopped dates. Cook on medium heat, stirring constantly, until all ingredients melt and blend well.

Remove from heat, add cereal, chopped pecans and vanilla and stir to mix well.

Roll into balls about ¾ inches in diameter.

Drop balls, a few at a time, into small grocery sack or plastic bag with enough powdered sugar to cover.

Shake lightly until date balls are coated with sugar. Store in airtight container.

Tip: These may be frozen.

Holly-Almond Cookies

1 cup (2 sticks) butter, softened
1 (3 ounce) package cream cheese, softened
1½ cups powdered sugar
2 cups flour
1 cup very finely chopped almonds
2 teaspoons almond flavoring
1 teaspoon vanilla
½ pound whole candied cherries

Preheat oven to 325°.

Cream butter, cream cheese and sugar, add flour and mix well.

Stir in almonds, almond flavoring and vanilla and mix well.

Take spoon of dough and form ball with your hands.

Punch a candied cherry in center of each ball (not to cover the cherry, just to flatten the cookie slightly).

Bake at 325° for 20 to 25 minutes or until edges are barely brown.

Fruit Balls

1½ pounds candied cherries
½ pound candied pineapple
1 (8 ounce) box pitted dates
1 (4 ounce) can angel flake coconut
4 cups chopped pecans
1 (14 ounce) can sweetened condensed milk

Preheat oven to 300°.

Chop cherries, pineapple and dates and mix well by hand.

Add coconut and pecans, pour condensed milk over mixture and mix well.

Put 1 teaspoon of mixture in miniature paper cups and place on cookie sheet.

Bake at 300° for 20 to 25 minutes and store in covered container.

Makes 150 to 200 fruit balls.

Tip: *These will keep in refrigerator for months if you can keep the family from eating them! My friend says it is not Christmas unless she makes these!*

Jingle Bell Cookies

Almost like candy!

1 cup sugar
½ cup (1 stick) butter
½ cup evaporated milk
1½ cups small marshmallows
1½ cups graham cracker crumbs or vanilla wafers
1 cup chopped pecans

Combine sugar, butter and evaporated milk in saucepan. Boil for 6 minutes, stirring constantly.

Remove from heat, add marshmallows and stir until marshmallows melt.

Stir in graham cracker crumbs and pecans. Hand beat until slightly cool and mixture becomes fairly stiff.

Quickly drop by tablespoonfuls onto buttered wax paper to cool. Store in covered container.

Cookies

Gum-Drop Chews

1 cup flour
½ teaspoon baking powder
½ teaspoon baking soda
⅛ teaspoon salt
1 egg
½ cup packed brown sugar
½ cup granulated sugar
½ cup (1 stick) butter, softened
1 teaspoon vanilla
2 cups gum drops, cut up
1 cup oats
1 cup chopped pecans

Preheat oven to 350°.

In mixing bowl, combine flour, baking powder, baking soda and salt.

Add egg, both sugars, butter and vanilla and mix well with dry ingredients.

Add gum drops, oats and pecans and mix. Drop by teaspoon on cookie sheet.

Bake at 350° for 12 to 15 minutes.

Tip: For a variation, use orange slices in place of gum drops.

Almond-Fudge Shortbread

1 cup (2 sticks) butter, softened
½ cup powdered sugar
¼ teaspoon salt
1¼ cups flour
1 (12 ounce) package chocolate chips
1 (14 ounce) can sweetened condensed milk
½ teaspoon almond extract
1 (2½ ounce) package almonds, toasted

Preheat oven to 350°. Grease 9 x 13-inch baking pan.

In mixing bowl, beat butter, sugar and salt.

Stir in flour, pat into prepared pan and bake for 15 minutes.

In medium saucepan over low heat, melt chocolate chips with sweetened condensed milk and stir constantly until chips melt.

Stir in almond extract, spread evenly over shortbread and sprinkle with almonds.

Chill several hours or until firm. Cut into bars. They may be stored at room temperature.

Tip: See page 172 for instructions to toast almonds.

Holiday Cookies

1 cup (2 sticks) butter, softened
¾ cup sugar
1 cup packed brown sugar
1 teaspoon vanilla
2 eggs
2½ cups flour
1 teaspoon baking soda
½ teaspoon salt
1 (12 ounce) package white chocolate chips
1 cup chopped pecans
1 (3½ ounce) can flaked coconut
20 red candied cherries, chopped
20 green candied cherries, chopped

Preheat oven to 350°.

In mixing bowl, cream butter, sugars, vanilla and eggs and beat well.

Add flour, baking soda and salt and mix well. Stir in chocolate chips, pecans, coconut and cherries.

Drop dough by teaspoon onto ungreased cookie sheet. (Dough will be very stiff.)

Bake at 350° for 8 to 10 minutes. Cool before storing.

Holiday Spritz Cookies

¾ cup (1¼ sticks) butter, softened
1¼ cups sugar
1 egg, well beaten
1 teaspoon almond flavoring
Food coloring (optional)
3 cups flour
1 teaspoon baking powder

Preheat oven to 350°.

Cream butter and sugar with mixer, add beaten egg and almond flavoring and beat well. Add food coloring.

Stir in flour and baking powder into creamed mixture.

Place dough in cookie press and press out desired shapes onto ungreased baking sheets.

Bake at 350° for about 8 minutes or until light brown.

Tip: Use some of decorative icings or sprinkles found in the grocery store to decorate your cookies.

Choc-O Cherry Cookies

A chocolate lover's delight!

½ cup (1 stick) butter, softened
1 cup sugar
1 egg
½ teaspoon vanilla
1½ cups flour
½ cup cocoa
¼ teaspoon salt
¼ teaspoon baking powder
¼ teaspoon baking soda
1 (10 ounce) jar maraschino cherries, well drained
1 (6 ounce) package chocolate chips

Preheat oven to 350°.

Cream butter, sugar, egg and vanilla until light and fluffy.

Add dry ingredients and mix.

Cut cherries in fourths, add cherries and chocolate chips and mix.

Drop by teaspoonfuls onto cookie sheet and bake at 350° for 15 minutes.

Holiday Cut-outs

6 tablespoons butter, softened
1 cup sugar
2 eggs
1 teaspoon vanilla
2½ cups flour
1 teaspoon baking powder
1 teaspoon salt
Powdered sugar for rolling dough

Preheat oven to 375°.

In large mixing bowl, combine butter, sugar, eggs and vanilla and beat until well blended and light and fluffy.

Add flour, baking powder and salt. Beat until all ingredients are well mixed.

Cover and chill dough in refrigerator for 1 hour.

Sprinkle powdered sugar on counter (cookies will not toughen as they might when rolled in flour). Roll dough ⅛-inch thick and cut into desired shapes.

Bake at 375° for 6 to 8 minutes. Remove immediately from cookie sheet and cool before decorating.

Tip: There is a wide variety of decorative icings already available on the grocery shelves. Many are in the tube so that even the smallest children can quickly become artists. Use your imagination!

Orange Fingers

Lovely for a fancy party!

3¼ cups vanilla wafer crumbs
1 (16 ounce) box powdered sugar
2 cups chopped pecans
1 (6 ounce) can frozen orange juice concentrate, thawed, undiluted
½ cup (1 stick) butter, melted
1 cup flaked coconut

Mix vanilla wafer crumbs, powdered sugar and pecans.

Stir in orange juice and butter.

Shape into 2-inch fingers, roll in coconut and chill.

Almond-Coconut Squares

You will think you are eating candy!

2 cups graham cracker crumbs
3 tablespoons brown sugar
½ cup (1 stick) butter, melted
1 (14 ounce) can sweetened condensed milk
1 (7 ounce) package flaked coconut
1 teaspoon vanilla

Topping:
1 (6 ounce) package chocolate chips
1 (6 ounce) package butterscotch chips
4 tablespoons (½ stick) butter
6 tablespoons chunky peanut butter
½ cup slivered almonds

Preheat oven to 325°.

Mix graham cracker crumbs, brown sugar and butter.

Pat into greased 9 x 13-inch baking pan.

Bake at 325° for 10 minutes and cool.

Combine sweetened condensed milk, coconut and vanilla. Pour over baked crust and bake another 25 minutes and cool.

For the topping, melt topping ingredients in top of double boiler.

Spread over baked ingredients. Cool and cut into squares.

Makes 3 dozen.

Candied Gingerbread

*The crystallized ginger is a fabulous addition
to an old-time favorite!*

1½ cups flour
1 teaspoon baking soda
1 teaspoon ground ginger
1 teaspoon cinnamon
½ cup (1 stick) butter, softened
¾ cup firmly packed brown sugar
2 eggs
¼ cup dark molasses
⅔ cup buttermilk
¼ cup chopped crystallized ginger

Preheat oven to 350°. Grease and flour 8-inch cake pan or
9-inch square pan.

Sift flour, baking soda and spices and set aside.

Beat butter until light and fluffy, add sugar and beat again. Add
eggs, beat well and stir in molasses.

Stir half dry ingredients into mixture, beat, add buttermilk and
beat again.

Add remaining dry ingredients. Fold in crystallized ginger. Pour
batter into prepared pan.

Bake at 350° for 45 minutes or until a tester inserted comes out
clean.

Cut in squares and serve warm with butter.

Coconut-Cherry Squares

This is not only pretty – it's good, good, good!

Pastry:
1⅓ cups flour
10 tablespoons (1¼ sticks) butter, softened
1½ cups powdered sugar

Filling:
3 eggs, beaten
1½ cups sugar
¾ cup flour
½ teaspoon salt
¾ teaspoon baking powder
1 teaspoon vanilla
¾ cup chopped pecans
¾ cup flaked coconut
¾ cup maraschino cherries, drained, chopped

Preheat oven to 350°.

In mixing bowl, combine pastry ingredients and press into bottom of 9 x 13-inch baking pan.

Bake at 350° for 20 minutes or just until golden and set aside.

Use same mixing bowl, combine filling ingredients and mix well.

Spread over crust and bake 25 minutes or until golden brown.

Cool and cut into squares.

Tip: You could give this an even more holiday look by using half green and half red maraschino cherries.

Pumpkin Crunch

I talked a bridge "buddy" out of this good recipe.

1 (16 ounce) can pumpkin
1 cup sugar
1 tablespoon pumpkin pie spice
3 eggs
½ teaspoon salt
1 (12 ounce) can evaporated milk
1 (18 ounce) yellow cake mix
½ cup (1 stick) butter, melted
1 cup chopped pecans

Preheat oven to 350°.

In mixing bowl, combine pumpkin, sugar, pie spice, eggs, salt and evaporated milk and beat well.

Pour into well greased and floured 9 x 13-inch baking dish.

Mix cake mix, melted butter and pecans to make a crumbly mixture. Spoon cake mixture over pumpkin mixture.

Bake at 350° for 35 to 40 minutes.

Tip: This is good served warm or cold.

Apricot-Almond Bars

1 (18 ounce) package yellow cake mix
½ (1 stick) butter, melted
¾ cup finely chopped almonds
1 (12 ounce) jar apricot preserves, divided, warmed
1 (8 ounce) package cream cheese, softened
¼ cup sugar
2 tablespoons flour
⅛ teaspoon salt
1 egg
1 teaspoon vanilla
⅔ cup flaked coconut

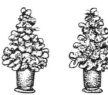

Preheat oven to 350°.

In large bowl, combine cake mix and butter and mix by hand just until crumbly.

Stir in almonds and reserve 1 cup crumb mixture. Lightly press remaining crumb mixture into greased 9 x 13-inch baking pan.

Carefully spread 1 cup preserves over crumb mixture, but leave a ¼-inch border.

Beat cream cheese with mixer until smooth. Add remaining preserves, sugar, flour, salt, egg and vanilla and beat well.

Carefully spread cream cheese mixture over top of preserves.

Combine reserved 1 cup crumb mixture and coconut and mix well. Sprinkle over cream cheese mixture.

Bake at 350° for 35 minutes or until center sets. Cool and store in refrigerator.

Iced-Pineapple Squares

1½ cups sugar
2 cups flour
1½ teaspoons baking soda
½ teaspoon salt
1 (20 ounce) can crushed pineapple with juice
2 eggs

Icing:
1½ cups sugar
½ cup (1 stick) butter
1 (5 ounce) can evaporated milk
1 cup chopped pecans
1 (7 ounce) can flaked coconut
1 teaspoon vanilla

Preheat oven to 350°.

Mix sugar, flour, baking soda, salt, pineapple and eggs and pour in 9 x 13-inch greased and floured pan.

Bake at 350° for about 35 minutes.

Cook icing as squares are baking. Mix sugar, butter and evaporated milk in saucepan and boil 4 minutes, stirring constantly.

Remove from heat and add pecans, coconut and vanilla. Spread over hot squares.

Serves 12.

Cookies

Glazed-Butterscotch Brownies

3 cups packed brown sugar
1 cup (2 sticks) butter, softened
3 eggs
3 cups flour
2 tablespoons baking powder
½ teaspoon salt
1½ cups chopped pecans
1 cup flaked coconut

Glaze:
½ cup packed brown sugar
⅓ cup evaporated milk
½ cup (1 stick) butter
⅛ teaspoon salt
1 cup powdered sugar
½ teaspoon vanilla

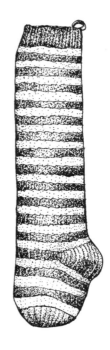

Preheat oven to 350°.

Combine and beat sugar and butter until fluffy; add eggs and blend.

Sift flour, baking powder and salt and add to other mixture 1 cup at a time. Add pecans and coconut.

Spread batter into large 11 x 17-inch well greased pan and bake at 350° for 20 to 25 minutes. (Batter will be hard to spread.)

For glaze: In saucepan, combine brown sugar, milk, butter and salt and bring to a boil.

Cool slightly and add powdered sugar and vanilla and beat until smooth. Spread over cooled brownies.

Butter-Pecan Turtle Bars

2 cups flour
¾ cup packed light brown sugar
½ cup (stick) butter, softened
1½ cups slightly chopped pecans
1 cup packed light brown sugar
½ cup plus 3 tablespoons (1⅓ sticks) butter
5 (1 ounce) squares semi-sweet chocolate
¼ cup (½ stick) butter

Preheat oven to 350°.

In large mixing bowl, combine flour, ¾ cup brown sugar and butter and blend until crumbly.

Pat firmly into greased 9 x 13-inch baking pan, sprinkle pecans over unbaked crust and set aside.

In small saucepan, combine 1 cup brown sugar and ½ cup plus 3 tablespoons (1⅓ sticks) butter. Cook over medium heat, stirring constantly. When mixture comes to a boil, boil for 1 minute, stirring constantly.

Drizzle caramel sauce over pecans and crust.

Bake at 350° for 18 minutes or until caramel layer is bubbly. Remove from oven and cool.

In saucepan, melt chocolate squares and butter and stir until smooth.

Pour over bars and spread around. Cool, cut into bars and chill.

Santa's Favorite Fudge

4½ cups sugar
1 (12 ounce) can evaporated milk
1 cup (2 sticks) butter
3 (6 ounce) packages chocolate chips
1 tablespoon vanilla
1½ cups chopped pecans

Bring sugar and milk to a rolling boil that cannot be stirred down. Boil for exactly 6 minutes, stirring constantly.

Remove from heat, add butter and chocolate chips and stir until they melt.

Add vanilla and pecans and stir well.

Pour into buttered 9 x 13-inch dish and let stand at least 6 hours or overnight before cutting.

Store in airtight container.

Divinity

2½ cups sugar
½ cup light corn syrup
½ cup water
¼ teaspoon salt
2 egg whites
1 teaspoon vanilla
1 cup chopped pecans

Mix sugar, corn syrup, water and salt in 2-quart saucepan. Cook over medium heat, stirring constantly, until mixture comes to a boil.

Reduce heat, cook without stirring, until temperature reaches 265° or until small amount of syrup forms a ball in cold water and holds its shape, yet is pliable.

Just before temperature reaches 265°, beat egg whites in large bowl until stiff peaks form when beater raises.

Beating constantly on high speed, very slowly pour hot syrup over egg whites.

Continue beating until small amount holds soft peaks when dropped from a spoon. Mix in vanilla and pecans. Work hurriedly and drop by teaspoonfuls onto wax paper.

Tip: It is better to wait for a sunny day to make divinity.

Candies

Date-Nut Loaf Candy

6 cups sugar
1 (12 ounce) can evaporated milk
½ cup white corn syrup
1 cup (2 sticks) butter
2 (8 ounce) boxes chopped dates
3 cups chopped pecans or English walnuts
1 tablespoon vanilla

In large saucepan, cook sugar, milk, corn syrup and butter until it boils about 5 minutes, stirring constantly with a wooden spoon or plastic spoon so mixture will not scorch.

Add dates and cook until it forms a soft ball in cup of cold water.

Take candy off heat and beat until it begins to get thick. Add pecans and vanilla and stir until real thick.

Spoon it out on wet cup towel to make a roll. This will make 2 rolls of candy. Let it stay wrapped until it is firm enough to slice.

Tip: Absolutely delicious! My good friend has made this for so many years that now she just "dumps" the ingredients in—without measuring! So she made up a special 'batch' and actually measured everything—just for this book!

Patience

Our Mom made this – so it's a special recipe!

1 cup milk
3 cups sugar, divided
2 tablespoons butter
1 teaspoon vanilla
1 cup chopped pecans

Heat milk and 2 cups sugar in saucepan.

Caramelize remaining 1 cup sugar in skillet.

Combine caramelized sugar with other mixture and cook until a soft ball forms in cold water.

Add butter and vanilla. Let sit in pan until slightly cool.

Beat until candy is dull and add pecans.

Pour into buttered pan or drop by teaspoonfuls.

Tip: Do not try to make this on a damp day.

Macadamia Candy

This is good, good, good!

2 (3 ounce) jars macadamia nuts
1 (20 ounce) package white almond bark, divided
¾ cup flaked coconut

Heat dry skillet over medium heat, toast nuts until slightly golden and set aside.

In double boiler, melt 12 squares white almond bark. (If you don't have a double boiler, just use a skillet to put water in and place the white almond bark in saucepan.)

As soon as almond bark melts, pour in macadamia nuts and coconut and stir well.

Place piece of wax paper on cookie sheet, pour candy on wax paper and spread out.

Chill 30 minutes to set. Break into pieces to serve.

Creamy Pralines

2¼ cups sugar
1 (3 ounce) can evaporated milk
½ cup white corn syrup
¼ teaspoon baking soda
¼ cup (½ stick) butter
1 teaspoon vanilla
2 cups pecans

In double boiler, combine sugar, evaporated milk, corn syrup and baking soda.

Cook, stirring constantly, until balls form when dropped into a cup of cold water or until it reaches the soft-ball stage on candy thermometer. This will take about 15 minutes.

Remove from heat, add butter, vanilla and pecans and beat until it is stiff enough to keep its shape when dropped on wax paper.

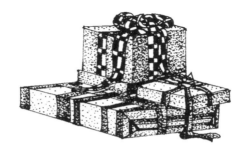

Toasted Almonds

This can be done in advance and frozen. It is great to have toasted, slivered almonds on hand. And, toasting lets the full flavor of the almonds stand out.

Preheat oven to 275°.

Place almonds in baking pan. Bake almonds for 15 minutes.

Chocolate-Dipped Strawberries

1 pint large strawberries with stems
1 (6 ounce) package milk chocolate chips
1 tablespoon shortening

Wash, dry and chill strawberries.

Melt chocolate chips and shortening in top of double boiler over hot water. Stir until smooth.

Hold each strawberry by stem and dip ¾ of the way into chocolate.

Place dipped strawberries on wax paper-lined baking sheet and chill.

These may be kept in refrigerator up to 4 hours before serving.

Popcorn Balls

3 quarts popped popcorn
1 cup sugar
½ cup water
⅓ cup light corn syrup
½ teaspoon salt
1 teaspoon vinegar
½ teaspoon vanilla
Green or red food coloring, optional

Boil sugar, water, corn syrup, salt and vinegar until hard-ball stage.

Add desired food coloring and vanilla and stir well. Pour over popcorn.

Butter hands lightly and shape into balls. Wrap each in plastic wrap.

Oat Munchies

This is great munching!

1 (16 ounce) package Quaker Oat Squares cereal
2 cups whole pecans
½ cup corn syrup
½ cup packed brown sugar
¼ cup (½ stick) butter
1 teaspoon vanilla
½ teaspoon baking soda

Preheat oven to 250°.

Combine cereal and pecans in 9 x 13-inch baking pan and set aside.

Combine corn syrup, brown sugar and butter in 2-cup bowl.

Microwave on HIGH 1½ minutes, stir and turn bowl.
Microwave on HIGH about 1 minute or until boiling.

Stir in vanilla and baking soda. Pour over cereal mixture, stirring well to coat evenly.

Bake in oven 1 hour and stir every 20 minutes. Spread on baking sheet to cool.

Crazy Cocoa Crisps

24 ounces white almond bark
2¼ cups chocolate, crispy rice cereal
2 cups dry roasted peanuts

Place almond bark in double boiler, heat stirring constantly, until almond bark melts.

Stir in cereal and peanuts. Drop by teaspoonful on cookie sheet.

Store in airtight container.

Hot-And-Sweet Mustard

This is a wonderful mustard to serve with ham or pork
and especially good on ham sandwiches!

4 ounces dry mustard
1 cup vinegar
3 eggs
1 cup sugar

Soak dry mustard in vinegar overnight.

Beat eggs and sugar and add to vinegar-mustard mixture.

In top of double boiler, cook over low heat for approximately 15 minutes, stirring constantly. Mixture will resemble a custard consistency.

Pour immediately into jars and seal. Store in refrigerator.

Christmas Morning Preserves

This is a delicacy. A very special treat.

2 cups dried apricots
2⅔ cups water
2 cups chunk pineapple with juice
2½ cups sugar
3 tablespoons lemon juice
1 (6 ounce) bottle red maraschino cherries
1 (6 ounce) bottle green maraschino cherries

Wash apricots and simmer for 30 minutes in just enough water to cover the apricots.

Add pineapple, pineapple juice, sugar and lemon juice and cook slowly, stirring often, until thick and clear, about 40 minutes.

Just before it is done, use potato masher to "mash" it up just a little.

Drain and halve cherries and add to mixture. Heat again, pour into hot sterilized jars and seal.

Process in boiling water bath for 20 minutes or keep in refrigerator to give each jar to a friend. They will be delighted with this gift!

Wine Jelly

Great served with pork!

2 cups white wine
½ cup water
½ cup lime juice
1 box Sure Jell
4¼ cups sugar

In saucepan large enough for jelly to bubble up while cooking, combine wine, water and lime juice. Bring to boiling point and stir in Sure Jell.

Add sugar, bring to a boiling point and boil for 1 minute.

Skim foam off jelly and pour into jelly jars. Seal with paraffin.

Tip: This works as an appetizer by putting a little cream cheese on a cracker and then top with a dab of the wine jelly!

Orange Pecans

1½ cups sugar
½ cup frozen orange juice concentrate
4 cups pecan halves

Cook sugar and orange juice concentrate until it is very bubbly and forms a soft ball in cup of water.

Pour in pecans and stir vigorously.

Pour on sheet of wax paper, spread pecans out and cool.

Break up in single halves.

Spiced Pecans

These will disappear! My friend made these for everybody in the bridge club. Now we expect them every Christmas.

2 cups sugar
½ cup water
2 teaspoons cinnamon
¼ teaspoon salt
1 teaspoon ground nutmeg
½ teaspoon ground cloves
4 cups pecan halves

Combine all ingredients except pecans in deep dish, mix well and cover with wax paper.

Microwave on HIGH for 4 minutes and stir. Microwave another 4 minutes.

Add pecans, quickly mix well and spread out on wax paper to cool.

Break apart and store in covered container.

Maple-Cinnamon Pecans

1 egg white
½ teaspoon cold water
½ teaspoon maple flavoring
2 cups pecan halves
⅔ cup sugar
¼ teaspoon salt
½ teaspoon cinnamon

Preheat oven to 225°.

Beat egg white, water and maple flavoring until frothy, but not stiff.

Add pecans and stir gently until pecans are well coated. Add sugar, salt and cinnamon and mix well.

Place on large pan or cookie sheet with sides.

Bake at 225° for 1 hour and stir every 15 minutes.

Holiday Potpourri

3 fresh juniper sprigs
2 red rosebuds
2 bay leaves
Cinnamon chips
2 cloves
Assorted pine cones
10 drops rose oil
3 drops pine oil
6 drops cinnamon oil
1 tablespoon orrisroot
Dried rose blossoms

Combine juniper sprigs, rosebuds, bay leaves, cinnamon, cloves and pine cones in big ceramic bowl.

In separate dish, mix the oils with orrisroot.

Stir this mixture into the first one and let mellow for a few weeks.

Place potpourri in dish and scatter the rose blossoms on top.

Something Green for Money –
Black-Eyed Peas for Luck

Cheesy Spinach

2 (10 ounce) packages frozen, chopped spinach
2 cups small-curd cottage cheese
2½ cups grated cheddar cheese
4 eggs, beaten
3 tablespoons flour
¼ cup (½ stick) butter, melted
¼ teaspoon garlic salt
¼ teaspoon lemon pepper
¼ teaspoon celery salt
1 teaspoon minced onion

Preheat oven to 325°.

Defrost spinach and squeeze out all water.

Mix spinach with remaining ingredients and place in
9 x 13-inch greased casserole.

Bake at 325° for 1 hour.

Serves 10.

Black-Eyed Pea Salad

2 (16 ounce) cans jalapeno black-eyed peas, drained
1 ripe avocado, peeled, chopped
½ purple onion, chopped
1 cup chopped celery
1 bell pepper, chopped

Dressing:
⅓ cup oil
⅓ cup white vinegar
3 tablespoons sugar
¼ teaspoon garlic powder
½ teaspoon salt

In large bowl, mix all salad ingredients.

Mix dressing ingredients, add dressing to vegetables, toss and chill.

Serves 10.

Index

Index

COOKBOOKS PUBLISHED BY COOKBOOK RESOURCES, LLC

The Ultimate Cooking With 4 Ingredients
4 Ingredient Recipes And 30-Minute Meals
Easy Cooking With 5 Ingredients
The Best of Cooking With 3 Ingredients
Easy Gourmet-Style Cooking With 5 Ingredients
Gourmet Cooking With 5 Ingredients
Healthy Cooking With 4 Ingredients
Easy Dessert Cooking With 5 Ingredients
Easy Slow-Cooker Cooking
Quick Fixes With Mixes
Casseroles To The Rescue
Kitchen Keepsakes/More Kitchen Keepsakes
Mother's Recipes
Recipe Keepsakes
Cookie Dough Secrets
Gifts For The Cookie Jar
Brownies In A Jar
101 Brownies
Cookie Jar Magic
Quilters' Cooking Companion
Classic Southern Cooking
Classic Tex-Mex and Texas Cooking
Classic Southwest Cooking
Classic Pennsylvania-Dutch Cooking
The Great Canadian Cookbook
The Best of Lone Star Legacy Cookbook
Lone Star Legacy
Lone Star Legacy II
Cookbook 25 Years
Pass The Plate
Authorized Texas Ranger Cookbook
Texas Longhorn Cookbook
Trophy Hunters' Guide To Cooking
Mealtimes and Memories
Holiday Recipes
Homecoming
Little Taste of Texas
Little Taste of Texas II
Texas Peppers
Southwest Sizzler
Southwest Ole
Class Treats
Leaving Home

cookbook
resources LLC
Bringing Family And Friends To The Table

www.cookbookresources.com